𝔈𝔡𝔦𝔱𝔦𝔬𝔫 𝔡𝔢 𝔏𝔲𝔵𝔢

THE WORKS

OF

ALFRED, LORD TENNYSON

𝔓𝔬𝔢𝔱 𝔏𝔞𝔲𝔯𝔢𝔞𝔱𝔢

EDITED BY WILLIAM J. ROLFE, LITT. D.

IN TWELVE VOLUMES

VOL. XI.

BOSTON
DANA ESTES & COMPANY
SUCCESSORS TO ESTES & LAURIAT
PUBLISHERS

CONTENTS.

Édition de Luxe.

LIST OF ILLUSTRATIONS.

VOL. XI.

QUEEN MARY:

A DRAMA.

DRAMATIS PERSONÆ.

QUEEN MARY.

PHILIP, *King of Naples and Sicily, afterwards King of Spain.*

THE PRINCESS ELIZABETH.

REGINALD POLE, *Cardinal and Papal Legate.*

SIMON RENARD, *Spanish Ambassador.*

LE SIEUR DE NOAILLES, *French Ambassador.*

THOMAS CRANMER, *Archbishop of Canterbury.*

SIR NICHOLAS HEATH, *Archbishop of York; Lord Chancellor after Gardiner.*

EDWARD COURTENAY, *Earl of Devon.*

LORD WILLIAM HOWARD, *afterwards Lord Howard, and Lord High Admiral.*

LORD WILLIAMS OF THAME.

LORD PAGET.

LORD PETRE.

STEPHEN GARDINER, *Bishop of Winchester and Lord Chancellor.*

EDMUND BONNER, *Bishop of London.*

THOMAS THIRLBY, *Bishop of Ely.*

SIR THOMAS WYATT
SIR THOMAS STAFFORD } *Insurrectionary Leaders.*

SIR RALPH BAGENHALL.

SIR ROBERT SOUTHWELL.

SIR HENRY BEDINGFIELD.

SIR WILLIAM CECIL.

SIR THOMAS WHITE, *Lord Mayor of London.*

THE DUKE OF ALVA
THE COUNT DE FERIA } *attending on Philip.*

PETER MARTYR.
FATHER COLE.
FATHER BOURNE.
VILLA GARCIA.
SOTO.
CAPTAIN BRETT } *Adherents of Wyatt.*
ANTHONY KNYVETT }
PETERS, *Gentleman of Lord Howard.*
ROGER, *Servant to Noailles.*
WILLIAM, *Servant to Wyatt.*
STEWARD OF HOUSEHOLD *to the Princess Elizabeth.*
OLD NOKES *and* NOKES.
MARCHIONESS OF EXETER, *Mother of Courtenay.*
LADY CLARENCE }
LADY MAGDALEN DACRES } *Ladies in Waiting to the Queen.*
ALICE. }
MAID OF HONOUR *to the Princess Elizabeth.*
JOAN } *two Country Wives.*
TIB }

Lords and other Attendants, Members of the Privy Council,
Members of Parliament, Two Gentlemen, Aldermen, Citizens,
Peasants, Ushers, Messengers, Guards, Pages, Gospellers,
Marshalmen, etc.

QUEEN MARY.

ACT I.

SCENE I. — ALDGATE RICHLY DECORATED.

CROWD. MARSHALMEN.

MARSHALMAN.

Stand back, keep a clear lane! When will her Majesty pass, sayst thou? why now, even now; wherefore draw back your heads and your horns before I break them, and make what noise you will with your tongues, so it be not treason. Long live Queen Mary, the lawful and legitimate daughter of Harry the Eighth! Shout, knaves!

CITIZENS.

Long live Queen Mary!

FIRST CITIZEN.

That's a hard word, legitimate; what does it mean?

SECOND CITIZEN.

It means a bastard.

THIRD CITIZEN.

Nay, it means true-born.

FIRST CITIZEN.

Why, did n't the Parliament make her a bastard?

SECOND CITIZEN.

No; it was the Lady Elizabeth.

THIRD CITIZEN.

That was after, man; that was after.

FIRST CITIZEN.

Then which is the bastard?

SECOND CITIZEN.

Troth, they be both bastards by Act of Parliament and Council.

THIRD CITIZEN.

Ay, the Parliament can make every true-born man of us a bastard. Old Nokes, can't it make thee a bastard? thou shouldst know, for thou art as white as three Christmases.

OLD NOKES (*dreamily*).

Who's a-passing?   King Edward or King
Richard?

THIRD CITIZEN.

No, old Nokes.

OLD NOKES.

It's Harry!

THIRD CITIZEN.

It's Queen Mary.

OLD NOKES.

The blessed Mary's a-passing!

[*Falls on his knees.*

NOKES.

Let father alone, my masters! he's past your
questioning.

THIRD CITIZEN.

Answer thou for him, then! thou 'rt no such
cockerel thyself, for thou was born i' the tail end
of old Harry the Seventh.

NOKES.

Eh! that was afore bastard-making began.   I
was born true man at five in the forenoon i' the
tail of old Harry, and so they can't make me a
bastard.

THIRD CITIZEN.

But if Parliament can make the Queen a bastard, why, it follows all the more that they can make thee one, who art fray'd i' the knees, and out at elbow, and bald o' the back, and bursten at the toes, and down at heels.

NOKES.

I was born of a true man and a ring'd wife, and I can't argue upon it; but I and my old woman 'ud burn upon it, that would we.

MARSHALMAN.

What are you cackling of bastardy under the Queen's own nose? I 'll have you flogg'd and burnt too, by the Rood I will.

FIRST CITIZEN.

He swears by the Rood. Whew!

SECOND CITIZEN.

Hark! the trumpets.

> [*The Procession passes,* MARY *and* ELIZABETH *riding side by side, and disappears under the gate.*

CITIZENS.

Long live Queen Mary! down with all traitors! God save her Grace; and death to Northumberland!   [*Exeunt.*

Manent TWO GENTLEMEN.

FIRST GENTLEMAN.

By God's light a noble creature, right royal!

SECOND GENTLEMAN.

She looks comelier than ordinary to-day; but
to my mind the Lady Elizabeth is the more
noble and royal.

FIRST GENTLEMAN.

I mean the Lady Elizabeth. Did you hear (I
have a daughter in her service who reported it)
that she met the Queen at Wanstead with five
hundred horse, and the Queen (tho' some say
they be much divided) took her hand, call'd her
sweet sister, and kiss'd not her alone, but all the
ladies of her following.

SECOND GENTLEMAN.

Ay, that was in her hour of joy; there will be
plenty to sunder and unsister them again: this

Gardiner for one, who is to be made Lord Chancellor, and will pounce like a wild beast out of
his cage to worry Cranmer.

FIRST GENTLEMAN.

And, furthermore, my daughter said that when
there rose a talk of the late rebellion, she spoke
even of Northumberland pitifully, and of the
good Lady Jane as a poor innocent child who
had but obeyed her father; and, furthermore,
she said that no one in her time should be burnt
for heresy.

SECOND GENTLEMAN.

Well, sir, I look for happy times.

FIRST GENTLEMAN.

There is but one thing against them.   I know
not if you know.

SECOND GENTLEMAN.

I suppose you touch upon the rumour that
Charles, the master of the world, has offer'd her
his son Philip, the Pope and the Devil.   I trust
it is but a rumour.

FIRST GENTLEMAN.

She is going now to the Tower to loose the
prisoners there, and among them Courtenay, to
be made Earl of Devon, of royal blood, of splendid feature, whom the council and all her people
wish her to marry. May it be so, for we are
many of us Catholics, but few Papists, and the
Hot Gospellers will go mad upon it.

SECOND GENTLEMAN.

Was she not betroth'd in her babyhood to the
Great Emperor himself?

FIRST GENTLEMAN.

Ay, but he's too old.

SECOND GENTLEMAN.

And again to her cousin Reginald Pole, now
Cardinal; but I hear that he too is full of aches
and broken before his day.

FIRST GENTLEMAN.

Oh, the Pope could dispense with his Cardina-
late, and his achage, and his breakage, if that
were all: will you not follow the procession?

SECOND GENTLEMAN.

No; I have seen enough for this day.

FIRST GENTLEMAN.

Well, I shall follow; if I can get near enough
I shall judge with my own eyes whether her Grace
incline to this splendid scion of Plantagenet.

[*Exeunt.*

SCENE II. A ROOM IN LAMBETH PALACE.

CRANMER.

To Strasburg, Antwerp, Frankfort, Zurich,
    Worms,
Geneva, Basle — our Bishops from their sees
Or fled, they say, or flying — Poinet, Barlow,
Bale, Scory, Coverdale; besides the Deans
Of Christchurch, Durham, Exeter, and Wells —
Ailmer and Bullingham, and hundreds more;
So they report: I shall be left alone.
No: Hooper, Ridley, Latimer, will not fly.

Enter PETER MARTYR.

PETER MARTYR.

Fly, Cranmer! were there nothing else, your
    name

Stands first of those who sign'd the Letters
        Patent
That gave her royal crown to Lady Jane.

CRANMER.

Stand first it may, but it was written last:
Those that are now her Privy Council sign'd
Before me: nay, the Judges had pronounced
That our young Edward might bequeath the
        crown
Of England, putting by his father's will.
Yet I stood out, till Edward sent for me.
The wan boy-king, with his fast-fading eyes
Fixt hard on mine, his frail transparent hand,
Damp with the sweat of death, and griping mine,
Whisper'd me, if I loved him, not to yield
His Church of England to the Papal wolf
And Mary; then I could no more — I sign'd.
Nay, for bare shame of inconsistency,
She cannot pass her traitor council by,
To make me headless.

PETER MARTYR.

                    That might be forgiven.
I tell you, fly, my lord. You do not own

The bodily presence in the Eucharist,
Their wafer and perpetual sacrifice:
Your creed will be your death.

CRANMER.

       Step after step,
Thro' many voices crying right and left,
Have I climb'd back into the primal church,
And stand within the porch, and Christ with me:
My flight were such a scandal to the faith,
The downfall of so many simple souls,
I dare not leave my post.

PETER MARTYR.

       But you divorced
Queen Catharine and her father; hence, her
  hate
Will burn till you are burn'd.

CRANMER.

       I cannot help it.
The Canonists and Schoolmen were with me.
'Thou shalt not wed thy brother's wife.' — 'T is
  written,
'They shall be childless.' True, Mary was born,

But France would not accept her for a bride
As being born from incest; and this wrought
Upon the King; and child by child, you know,
Were momentary sparkles, out as quick
Almost as kindled; and he brought his doubts
And fears to me.   Peter, I'll swear for him
He *did* believe the bond incestuous.
But wherefore am I trenching on the time
That should already have seen your steps a
        mile
From me and Lambeth?   God be with you! Go.

PETER MARTYR.

Ah, but how fierce a letter you wrote against
Their superstition when they slander'd you
For setting up a mass at Canterbury
To please the Queen.

CRANMER.

                It was a wheedling monk
Set up the mass.

PETER MARTYR.

                I know it, my good lord.
But you so bubbled over with hot terms

Of Satan, liars, blasphemy, Antichrist,
She never will forgive you.   Fly, my lord, fly!

CRANMER.

I wrote it, and God grant me power to burn!

PETER MARTYR.

They have given me a safe conduct: for all that
I dare not stay.   I fear, I fear, I see you,
Dear friend, for the last time; farewell, and fly.

CRANMER.

Fly and farewell, and let me die the death.
                    [*Exit* PETER MARTYR.

Enter OLD SERVANT.

Oh, kind and gentle master, the Queen's Officers
Are here in force to take you to the Tower.

CRANMER.

Ay, gentle friend, admit them.   I will go.
I thank my God it is too late to fly.
                    [*Exeunt.*

SCENE III. — St. Paul's Cross.

FATHER BOURNE *in the pulpit. A crowd.*
MARCHIONESS OF EXETER, COURTENAY. *The*
SIEUR DE NOAILLES *and his man* ROGER *in*
front of the stage. Hubbub.

NOAILLES.

Hast thou let fall those papers in the palace?

ROGER.

Ay, sir.

NOAILLES.

'There will be no peace for Mary till Elizabeth
    lose her head.'

ROGER.

Ay, sir.

NOAILLES.

And the other, 'Long live Elizabeth the
    Queen!'

ROGER.

Ay, sir; she needs must tread upon them.

NOAILLES.

                                        Well.

These beastly swine make such a grunting here,
I cannot catch what Father Bourne is saying.

ROGER.

Quiet a moment, my masters; hear what the
shaveling has to say for himself.

CROWD.

Hush — hear!

BOURNE.

— and so this unhappy land, long divided in
itself, and sever'd from the faith, will return into
the one true fold, seeing that our gracious
Virgin Queen hath —

CROWD.

No pope! no pope!

ROGER (*to those about him, mimicking* BOURNE).

— hath sent for the holy legate of the holy
father the Pope, Cardinal Pole, to give us all
that holy absolution which —

FIRST CITIZEN.

Old Bourne to the life!

SECOND CITIZEN.

Holy absolution! holy Inquisition!

Third Citizen.

Down with the Papist!   [*Hubbub.*

Bourne.

— and now that your good bishop, Bonner,
who hath lain so long under bonds for the
faith —   [*Hubbub.*

Noailles.

Friend Roger, steal thou in among the crowd,
And get the swine to shout ' Elizabeth.'
Yon gray old Gospeller, sour as mid-winter,
Begin with him.

Roger (*goes*).

By the mass, old friend, we 'll have no pope
here while the Lady Elizabeth lives.

Gospeller.

Art thou of the true faith, fellow, that swearest
by the mass?

Roger.

Ay, that am I, new converted, but the old
leaven sticks to my tongue yet.

FIRST CITIZEN.

He says right; by the mass, we'll have no
mass here.

VOICES OF THE CROWD.

Peace! hear him; let his own words damn
the Papist. From thine own mouth I judge
thee — tear him down!

BOURNE.

— and since our Gracious Queen, let me call
her our second Virgin Mary, hath begun to
re-edify the true temple —

FIRST CITIZEN.

Virgin Mary! we'll have no virgins here —
we'll have the Lady Elizabeth!

> [*Swords are drawn, a knife is hurled and
> sticks in the pulpit. The mob throng to
> the pulpit stairs.*

MARCHIONESS OF EXETER.

Son Courtenay, wilt thou see the holy father
Murdered before thy face? up, son, and save
    him!
They love thee, and thou canst not come to
    harm.

COURTENAY (*in the pulpit*).

Shame, shame, my masters! are you English-
    born,
And set yourselves by hundreds against one?

CROWD.

A Courtenay! a Courtenay!
    [*A train of Spanish servants crosses at the
    back of the stage.*

NOAILLES.

These birds of passage come before their
    time:
Stave off the crowd upon the Spaniard there.

ROGER.

My masters, yonder's fatter game for you
Than this old gaping gurgoyle: look you
    there —
The Prince of Spain coming to wed our Queen!
After him, boys! and pelt him from the city.
    [*They seize stones and follow the Spaniards.
    Exeunt on the other side* MARCHIONESS OF
    EXETER *and* ATTENDANTS.

NOAILLES (*to* ROGER).

Stand from me.   If Elizabeth lose her head —
That makes for France.
And if her people, anger'd thereupon,
Arise against her and dethrone the Queen —
That makes for France.
And if I breed confusion anyway —
That makes for France.

    Good-day, my Lord of Devon;
A bold heart yours to beard that raging mob!

COURTENAY.

My mother said, Go up; and up I went.
I knew they would not do me any wrong,
For I am mighty popular with them, Noailles.

NOAILLES.

You look'd a king.

COURTENAY.

    Why not?   I am king's blood.

NOAILLES.

And in the whirl of change may come to be
  one.

Courtenay.

Ah!

Noailles.

But does your gracious Queen entreat you
    kinglike?

Courtenay.

'Fore God, I think she entreats me like a child.

Noailles.

You've but a dull life in this maiden court,
I fear, my Lord?

Courtenay.

    A life of nods and yawns.

Noailles.

So you would honour my poor house to-night,
We might enliven you.   Divers honest fellows,
The Duke of Suffolk lately freed from prison,
Sir Peter Carew and Sir Thomas Wyatt,
Sir Thomas Stafford, and some more — we play.

Courtenay.

At what?

Noailles.

The Game of Chess.

COURTENAY.

The Game of Chess !
I can play well, and I shall beat you there.

NOAILLES.

Ay, but we play with Henry, King of France,
And certain of his court.
His Highness makes his moves across the
   Channel,
We answer him with ours, and there are
   messengers
That go between us.

COURTENAY.

Why, such a game, sir, were whole years a-
   playing.

NOAILLES.

Nay; not so long I trust.   That all depends
Upon the skill and swiftness of the players.

COURTENAY.

The King is skilful at it?

NOAILLES.

Very, my Lord.

COURTENAY.

And the stakes high?

NOAILLES.

But not beyond your means.

COURTENAY.

Well, I'm the first of players.   I shall win.

NOAILLES.

With our advice and in our company,
And so you well attend to the King's moves,
I think you may.

COURTENAY.

When do you meet?

NOAILLES.

To-night.

COURTENAY (*aside*).

I will be there; the fellow's at his tricks —
Deep — I shall fathom him.   (*Aloud.*)   Good
morning, Noailles.

[*Exit* Courtenay.

NOAILLES.

Good-day, my Lord.   Strange game of chess!
    a King
That with her own pawns plays against a Queen,
Whose play is all to find herself a King.
Ay; but this fine blue-blooded Courtenay seems
Too princely for a pawn.   Call him a Knight,
That, with an ass's, not a horse's head,
Skips every way, from levity or from fear.
Well, we shall use him somehow, so that
    Gardiner
And Simon Renard spy not out our game
Too early.   Roger, thinkest thou that any one
Suspected thee to be my man?

ROGER.
                    Not one, sir.

NOAILLES.
No! the disguise was perfect.   Let 's away.
                    [*Exeunt.*

SCENE IV.

LONDON.   A ROOM IN THE PALACE.

ELIZABETH.   *Enter* COURTENAY.

COURTENAY.

So yet am I,
Unless my friends and mirrors lie to me,
A goodlier-looking fellow than this Philip.
Pah!
The Queen is ill advised: shall I turn traitor?
They've almost talked me into it: yet the word
Affrights me somewhat: to be such a one
As Harry Bolingbroke hath a lure in it.
Good now, my Lady Queen, tho' by your age
And by your looks you are not worth the having,
Yet by your crown you are.

　　　　　　　　　　[*Seeing* ELIZABETH.
　　　　　　　　The Princess there?
If I tried her, and la — she's amorous.
Have we not heard of her in Edward's time,
Her freaks and frolics with the late Lord Admiral?

I do believe she'd yield.   I should be still
A party in the state; and then, who knows —

ELIZABETH.
What are you musing on, my Lord of Devon?

COURTENAY.
Has not the Queen —

ELIZABETH.
Done what, Sir?

COURTENAY.
                 — made you follow
The Lady Suffolk and the Lady Lennox? —
You,
The heir presumptive.

ELIZABETH.
Why do you ask? you know it.

COURTENAY.
You needs must bear it hardly.

ELIZABETH.
                No, indeed!
I am utterly submissive to the Queen.

COURTENAY.

Well, I was musing upon that; the Queen
Is both my foe and yours: we should be friends.

ELIZABETH.

My Lord, the hatred of another to us
Is no true bond of friendship.

COURTENAY.

       Might it not
Be the rough preface of some closer bond?

ELIZABETH.

My Lord, you late were loosed from out the
  Tower,
Where, like a butterfly in a chrysalis,
You spent your life; that broken, out you flutter
Thro' the new world, go zigzag, now would settle
Upon this flower, now that; but all things here
At court are known; you have solicited
The Queen, and been rejected.

COURTENAY.

       Flower, she!
Half faded! but you, cousin, are fresh and sweet
As the first flower no bee has ever tried.

ELIZABETH.

Are you the bee to try me? why, but now
I called you butterfly.

COURTENAY.

You did me wrong,
I love not to be called a butterfly:
Why do you call me butterfly?

ELIZABETH.

Why do you go so gay then?

COURTENAY.

Velvet and gold.
This dress was made me as the Earl of Devon
To take my seat in; looks it not right royal?

ELIZABETH.

So royal that the Queen forbade you wearing it.

COURTENAY.

I wear it then to spite her.

ELIZABETH.

My Lord, my Lord,
I see you in the Tower again. Her Majesty
Hears you affect the Prince — prelates kneel to
        you. —

COURTENAY.

I am the noblest blood in Europe, Madam,
A Courtenay of Devon, and her cousin.

ELIZABETH.

She hears you make your boast that after all
She means to wed you.   Folly, my good Lord.

COURTENAY.

How folly? a great party in the state
Wills me to wed her.

ELIZABETH.

　　　　　　　Failing her, my Lord,
Doth not as great a party in the state
Will you to wed me?

COURTENAY.

　　　　　　Even so, fair lady.

ELIZABETH.

You know to flatter ladies.

COURTENAY.

　　　　　　Nay, I meant
True matters of the heart.

ELIZABETH.

                    My heart, my Lord,
Is no great party in the state as yet.

COURTENAY.

Great, said you? nay, you shall be great. I
    love you,
Lay my life in your hands. Can you be close?

ELIZABETH.

Can you, my Lord?

COURTENAY.

                Close as a miser's casket.
Listen:
The King of France, Noailles the Ambassador,
The Duke of Suffolk and Sir Peter Carew,
Sir Thomas Wyatt, I myself, some others,
Have sworn this Spanish marriage shall not be.
If Mary will not hear us — well — conjecture —
Were I in Devon with my wedded bride,
The people there so worship me — Your ear;
You shall be Queen.

ELIZABETH.

             You speak too low, my Lord;
I cannot hear you.

COURTENAY.

I 'll repeat it.

ELIZABETH.

No!

Stand further off, or you may lose your head.

COURTENAY.

I have a head to lose for your sweet sake.

ELIZABETH.

Have you, my Lord?   Best keep it for your own.
Nay, pout not, cousin.
Not many friends are mine, except indeed
Among the many.   I believe you mine;
And so you may continue mine, farewell,
And that at once.

Enter MARY, *behind.*

MARY.

Whispering — leagued together
To bar me from my Philip.

COURTENAY.

Pray — consider —

ELIZABETH (*seeing the* QUEEN).

Well, that's a noble horse of yours, my Lord.
I trust that he will carry you well to-day,
And heal your headache.

COURTENAY.

You are wild; what headache?
Heartache, perchance; not headache.

ELIZABETH (*aside to* COURTENAY).

Are you blind?
[COURTENAY *sees the* QUEEN *and exit.*
Exit MARY.

Enter LORD WILLIAM HOWARD.

HOWARD.

Was that my Lord of Devon? do not you
Be seen in corners with my Lord of Devon.
He hath fallen out of favour with the Queen.
She fears the Lords may side with you and
    him
Against her marriage; therefore is he dangerous.
And if this Prince of fluff and feather come
To woo you, niece, he is dangerous everyway.

ELIZABETH.

Not very dangerous that way, my good uncle.

HOWARD.

But your own state is full of danger here.
The disaffected, heretics, reformers,
Look to you as the one to crown their ends.
Mix not yourself with any plot I pray you;
Nay, if by chance you hear of any such,
Speak not thereof — no, not to your best friend,
Lest you should be confounded with it.   Still —
Perinde ac cadaver — as the priest says,
You know your Latin — quiet as a dead body.
What was my Lord of Devon telling you?

ELIZABETH.

Whether he told me anything or not,
I follow your good counsel, gracious uncle.
Quiet as a dead body.

HOWARD.

                You do right well.
I do not care to know; but this I charge you,
Tell Courtenay nothing.   The Lord Chancellor
(I count it as a kind of virtue in him,

He hath not many), as a mastiff dog
May love a puppy cur for no more reason
Than that the twain have been tied up together,
Thus Gardiner — for the two were fellow-pris-
    oners
So many years in yon accursed Tower —
Hath taken to this Courtenay. Look to it,
    niece,
He hath no fence when Gardiner questions him;
All oozes out; yet him — because they know
    him
The last White Rose, the last Plantagenet
(Nay, there is Cardinal Pole, too), the people
Claim as their natural leader — ay, some say
That you shall marry him, make him King
    belike.

ELIZABETH.

Do they say so, good uncle?

HOWARD.

                  Ay, good niece!
You should be plain and open with me, niece.
You should not play upon me.

ELIZABETH.

No, good uncle.

Enter GARDINER.

GARDINER.

The Queen would see your Grace upon the
moment.

ELIZABETH.

Why, my lord Bishop?

GARDINER.

I think she means to counsel your withdrawing
To Ashridge, or some other country house.

ELIZABETH.

Why, my lord Bishop?

GARDINER.

I do but bring the message, know no more.
Your Grace will hear her reasons from herself.

ELIZABETH.

'T is mine own wish fulfill'd before the word
Was spoken, for in truth I had meant to crave
Permission of her Highness to retire
To Ashridge, and pursue my studies there.

Gardiner.

Madam, to have the wish before the word
Is man's good fairy — and the Queen is yours.
I left her with rich jewels in her hand,
Whereof 't is like enough she means to make
A farewell present to your Grace.

Elizabeth.

       My Lord,
I have the jewel of a loyal heart.

Gardiner.

I doubt it not, Madam, most loyal.
       [*Bows low and exit.*

Howard.

       See,
This comes of parleying with my Lord of
  Devon.
Well, well, you must obey ; and I myself
Believe it will be better for your welfare.
Your time will come.

Elizabeth.

     I think my time will come.
Uncle,

I am of sovereign nature, that I know,
Not to be quell'd; and I have felt within me
Stirrings of some great doom when God's just
     hour
Peals — but this fierce old Gardiner — his big
     baldness,
That irritable forelock which he rubs,
His buzzard beak and deep-incavern'd eyes
Half fright me.

HOWARD.

        You 've a bold heart; keep it so.
He cannot touch you save that you turn traitor;
And so take heed I pray you — you are one
Who love that men should smile upon you,
     niece.
They 'd smile you into treason — some of them.

ELIZABETH.

I spy the rock beneath the smiling sea.
But if this Philip, the proud Catholic prince,
And this bald priest, and she that hates me,
     seek
In that lone house to practise on my life,
By poison, fire, shot, stab —

HOWARD.

                They will not, niece.
Mine is the fleet and all the power at sea —
Or will be in a moment.   If they dared
To harm you, I would blow this Philip and all
Your trouble to the dog-star and the devil.

ELIZABETH.

To the Pleiads, uncle; they have lost a sister.

HOWARD.

But why say that? what have you done to lose
    her?
Come, come, I will go with you to the Queen.
                           [Exeunt.

SCENE V. — A ROOM IN THE PALACE.

MARY *with* PHILIP'S *miniature.*   ALICE.

MARY (*kissing the miniature*).

Most goodly, kinglike, and an emperor's son, —
A king to be, — is he not noble, girl?

ALICE.

Goodly enough, your Grace, and yet, methinks,
I have seen goodlier.

MARY.

                    Ay ; some waxen doll
Thy baby eyes have rested on, belike ;
All red and white, the fashion of our land.
But my good mother came (God rest her soul!)
Of Spain, and I am Spanish in myself,
And in my likings.

ALICE.

                    By your Grace's leave,
Your royal mother came of Spain, but took
To the English red and white. Your royal
        father
(For so they say) was all pure lily and rose
In his youth, and like a lady.

MARY.
                            O just God!
Sweet mother, you had time and cause enough
To sicken of his lilies and his roses.
Cast off, betray'd, defamed, divorced, forlorn!
And then the King — that traitor past forgive-
        ness,
The false archbishop fawning on him, married
The mother of Elizabeth — a heretic

Even as *she* is; but God hath sent me here
To take such order with all heretics
That it shall be, before I die, as tho'
My father and my brother had not lived.
What wast thou saying of this Lady Jane,
Now in the Tower?

ALICE.

    Why, Madam, she was passing
Some chapel down in Essex, and with her
Lady Anne Wharton, and the Lady Anne
Bow'd to the Pyx; but Lady Jane stood up
Stiff as the very backbone of heresy.
And wherefore bow ye not, says Lady Anne,
To him within there who made heaven and
   earth?
I cannot, and I dare not, tell your Grace
What Lady Jane replied.

MARY.

     But I will have it.
ALICE.

She said — pray pardon me, and pity her —
She hath hearken'd evil counsel — ah! she said
The baker made him.

MARY.

Monstrous! blasphemous!

She ought to burn.   Hence, thou (*Exit* Alice).

No — being traitor

Her head will fall: shall it? she is but a child.

We do not kill the child for doing that

His father whipt him into doing — a head

So full of grace and beauty! would that mine

Were half as gracious!   Oh, my lord to be,

My love, for thy sake only!

I am eleven years older than he is.

But will he care for that?

No, by the holy Virgin, being noble,

But love me only: then the bastard sprout,

My sister, is far fairer than myself.

Will he be drawn to her?

No, being of the true faith with myself.

Paget is for him — for to wed with Spain

Would treble England — Gardiner is against
      him;

The Council, people, Parliament against him;

But I will have him!   My hard father hated me;

My brother rather hated me than loved;

My sister cowers and hates me.   Holy Virgin,
Plead with thy blessed Son; grant me my
      prayer :
Give me my Philip ; and we two will lead
The living waters of the Faith again
Back thro' their widow'd channel here, and
      watch
The parch'd banks rolling incense, as of old,
To heaven, and kindled with the palms of
      Christ !
              (*Enter* USHER.)
Who waits, sir?
            USHER.
          Madam, the Lord Chancellor.

            MARY.

Bid him come in. (*Enter* GARDINER.)   Good
      morning, my good Lord.
                [*Exit* USHER.
        GARDINER.
That every morning of your Majesty
May be most good, is every morning's prayer
Of your most loyal subject, Stephen Gardiner.

            MARY.
Come you to tell me this, my Lord?

Gardiner.
And more.

Your people have begun to learn your worth.

Your pious wish to pay King Edward's debts,

Your lavish household curb'd, and the re-
mission

Of half that subsidy levied on the people,

Make all tongues praise and all hearts beat for
you.

I'd have you yet more loved: the realm is
poor,

The exchequer at neap-tide: we might withdraw

Part of our garrison at Calais.

Mary.
Calais!

Our one point on the main, the gate of France!

I am Queen of England; take mine eyes, mine
heart,

But do not lose me Calais.

Gardiner.
Do not fear it.

Of that hereafter.   I say your Grace is loved.

That I may keep you thus, who am your friend
And ever faithful counsellor, might I speak?

Mary.

I can forespeak your speaking.   Would I marry
Prince Philip, if all England hate him?   That is
Your question, and I front it with another:
Is it England, or a party?   Now, your answer.

Gardiner.

My answer is, I wear beneath my dress
A shirt of mail: my house hath been assaulted,
And when I walk abroad the populace,
With fingers pointed like so many daggers,
Stab me in fancy, hissing Spain and Philip;
And when I sleep a hundred men-at-arms
Guard my poor dreams for England.   Men would
         murder me,
Because they think me favourer of this marriage.

Mary.

And that were hard upon you, my Lord Chan-
     cellor.

Gardiner.

But our young Earl of Devon —

MARY.

                              Earl of Devon?
I freed him from the Tower, placed him at
     Court;
I made him Earl of Devon, and — the fool —
He wrecks his health and wealth on courtesans,
And rolls himself in carrion like a dog.

GARDINER.

More like a school-boy that hath broken bounds
Sickening himself with sweets.

MARY.

                         I will not hear of him.
Good, then, they will revolt: but I am Tudor,
And shall control them.

GARDINER.

                         I will help you, Madam,
Even to the utmost.   All the church is grateful.
You have ousted the mock priest, repulpited
The shepherd of Saint Peter, raised the rood
     again,
And brought us back the mass. I am all thanks
To God and to your Grace: yet I know well,

Your people, and I go with them so far,
Will brook nor Pope nor Spaniard here to play
The tyrant, or in commonwealth or church.

MARY (*showing the picture*).
Is this the face of one who plays the tyrant?
Peruse it; is it not goodly, ay, and gentle?

GARDINER.
Madam, methinks a cold face and a haughty.
And when your Highness talks of Courtenay —
Ay, true — a goodly one.   I would his life
Were half as goodly (*aside*).

MARY.
            What is that you mutter?

GARDINER.
Oh, Madam, take it bluntly; marry Philip,
And be stepmother of a score of sons!
The prince is known in Spain, in Flanders, ha!
For Philip —
            MARY.
            You offend us; you may leave us.
You see thro' warping glasses.

GARDINER.

If your Majesty —

MARY.

I have sworn upon the body and blood of Christ
I 'll none but Philip.

GARDINER.

Hath your Grace so sworn?

MARY.

Ay, Simon Renard knows it.

GARDINER.

News to me!
It then remains for your poor Gardiner,
So you still care to trust him somewhat less
Than Simon Renard, to compose the event
In some such form as least may harm your
    Grace.

MARY.

I 'll have the scandal sounded to the mud.
I know it a scandal.

GARDINER.

All my hope is now
It may be found a scandal.

MARY.

You offend us.

GARDINER (*aside*).

These princes are like children, must be phys-
    ick'd,
The bitter in the sweet.   I have lost mine office,
It may be, thro' mine honesty, like a fool.

[*Exit.*

Enter USHER.

MARY.

Who waits?

USHER.

The Ambassador from France, your Grace.

MARY (*sits down*).

Bid him come in.   Good morning, Sir de
    Noailles.   [*Exit* USHER.

NOAILLES (*entering*).

A happy morning to your Majesty.

MARY.

And I should some time have a happy morning;
I have had none yet.   What says the King your
    master?

NOAILLES.

Madam, my master hears with much alarm
That you may marry Philip, Prince of Spain —
Foreseeing, with whate'er unwillingness,
That if this Philip be the titular King
Of England, and at war with him, your Grace
And kingdom will be suck'd into the war,
Ay, tho' you long for peace; wherefore, my
        master,
If but to prove your Majesty's goodwill,
Would fain have some fresh treaty drawn be-
        tween you.

MARY.

Why some fresh treaty? wherefore should I
        do it?
Sir, if we marry, we shall still maintain
All former treaties with his Majesty.
Our royal word for that! and your good master,
Pray God he do not be the first to break them,
Must be content with that; and so, farewell.

NOAILLES (*going, returns*).

I would your answer had been other, Madam,
For I foresee dark days.

MARY.

            And so do I, sir;
Your master works against me in the dark.
I do believe he holp Northumberland
Against me.

NOAILLES.

       Nay, pure phantasy, your Grace.
Why should he move against you?

MARY.

          Will you hear why?
Mary of Scotland, — for I have not own'd
My sister, and I will not, — after me
Is heir of England; and my royal father,
To make the crown of Scotland one with ours,
Had mark'd her for my brother Edward's bride;
Ay, but your king stole her a babe from Scot-
    land
In order to betroth her to your Dauphin.
See then:
Mary of Scotland, married to your Dauphin,
Would make our England, France;
Mary of England, joining hands with Spain,
Would be too strong for France.

Yea, were there issue born to her, Spain and we,
One crown, might rule the world.   There lies
    your fear.
That is your drift.   You play at hide and seek.
Show me your faces!

NOAILLES.

         Madam, I am amazed:
French, I must needs wish all good things for
    France.
That must be pardon'd me ; but I protest
Your Grace's policy hath a farther flight
Than mine into the future.   We but seek
Some settled ground for peace to stand upon.

MARY.

Well, we will leave all this, sir, to our council.
Have you seen Philip ever?

NOAILLES.

              Only once.

MARY.

Is this like Philip?

NOAILLES.

         Ay, but nobler-looking.

MARY.

Hath he the large ability of the Emperor?

NOAILLES.

No, surely.

MARY.

I can make allowance for thee,
Thou speakest of the enemy of thy king.

NOAILLES.

Make no allowance for the naked truth.
He is every way a lesser man than Charles;
Stone-hard, ice-cold — no dash of daring in
    him.

MARY.

If cold, his life is pure.

NOAILLES.

Why (*smiling*), no, indeed.

MARY.

Sayst thou?

NOAILLES.

A very wanton life indeed (*smiling*).

MARY.

Your audience is concluded, sir.

[*Exit* NOAILLES.

                              You cannot
Learn a man's nature from his natural foe.

                    Enter Usher.
Who waits?
                    Usher.
The Ambassador of Spain, your Grace. [*Exit.*

              Enter Simon Renard.

          Mary (*rising to meet him*).
Thou art ever welcome, Simon Renard. Hast
      thou
Brought me the letter which thine Emperor
      promised
Long since, a formal offer of the hand
Of Philip?
                    Renard.
          Nay, your Grace, it hath not reach'd me.
I know not wherefore — some mischance of
      flood,
And broken bridge, or spavin'd horse, or wave
And wind at their old battle: he must have
      written.
                    Mary.
But Philip never writes me one poor word,
Which in his absence had been all my wealth.
Strange in a wooer!

RENARD.

                    Yet I know the Prince,
So your king-parliament suffer him to land,
Yearns to set foot upon your island shore.

MARY.

God change the pebble which his kingly foot
First presses into some more costly stone
Than ever blinded eye!   I'll have one mark it
And bring it me.   I'll have it burnish'd firelike;
I'll set it round with gold, with pearl, with
          diamond.
Let the great angel of the church come with
          him,
Stand on the deck and spread his wings for sail!
God lay the waves and strow the storms at sea,
And here at land among the people!   O Renard,
I am much beset, I am almost in despair.
 Paget is ours.   Gardiner perchance is ours;
But for our heretic Parliament —

RENARD.

                    O Madam,
You fly your thoughts like kites.   My master,
          Charles,

Bade you go softly with your heretics here,
Until your throne had ceased to tremble.   Then
Spit them like larks for aught I care.   Besides,
When Henry broke the carcase of your church
To pieces, there were many wolves among you
Who dragg'd the scatter'd limbs into their den.
The Pope would have you make them render
     these;
So would your cousin, Cardinal Pole; ill counsel!
These let them keep at present; stir not yet
This matter of the Church lands.   At his coming
Your star will rise.

                MARY.

                My star! a baleful one.
I see but the black night, and hear the wolf.
What star?

             RENARD.

          Your star will be your princely son,
Heir of this England and the Netherlands!
And if your wolf the while should howl for
     more,
We'll dust him from a bag of Spanish gold.
I do believe — I have dusted some already —
That, soon or late, your Parliament is ours.

MARY.

Why do they talk so foully of your Prince,
Renard?

RENARD.

The lot of Princes.   To sit high
Is to be lied about.

MARY.

They call him cold,
Haughty, ay, worse.

RENARD.

Why, doubtless, Philip shows
Some of the bearing of your blue blood — still
All within measure — nay, it well becomes him.

MARY.

Hath he the large ability of his father?

RENARD.

Nay, some believe that he will go beyond him.

MARY.

Is this like him?

RENARD.

Ay, somewhat; but your Philip
Is the most princelike Prince beneath the sun.
This is a daub to Philip.

MARY.

Of a pure life?

RENARD.

As an angel among angels.   Yea, by Heaven,
The text — Your Highness knows it, 'Whoso-
    ever
Looketh after a woman,' would not graze
The Prince of Spain.   You are happy in him
    there,
Chaste as your Grace!

MARY.

I am happy in him there.

RENARD.

And would be altogether happy, Madam,
So that your sister were but look'd to closer.
You have sent her from the court, but then she
    goes,
I warrant, not to hear the nightingales,
But hatch you some new treason in the woods.

MARY.

We have our spies abroad to catch her tripping,
And then if caught, to the Tower.

RENARD.

               The Tower! the block!
The word has turn'd your Highness pale; the
    thing
Was no such scarecrow in your father's time.
I have heard, the tongue yet quiver'd with the
    jest
When the head leapt — so common! I do think,
To save your crown, that it must come to this.

MARY.

No, Renard; it must never come to this.

RENARD.

Not yet; but your old Traitors of the Tower —
Why, when you put Northumberland to death,
The sentence having passed upon them all,
Spared you the Duke of Suffolk, Guildford
    Dudley,
Even that young girl who dared to wear your
    crown?

MARY.

Dared? nay, not so; the child obey'd her
    father.
Spite of her tears her father forced it on her.

RENARD.

Good Madam, when the Roman wish'd to reign,
He slew not him alone who wore the purple,
But his assessor in the throne, perchance
A child more innocent than Lady Jane.

MARY.

I am English Queen, not Roman Emperor.

RENARD.

Yet too much mercy is a want of mercy,
And wastes more life. Stamp out the fire, or
        this
Will smoulder and re-flame, and burn the throne
Where you should sit with Philip: he will not
        come
Till she be gone

MARY.

                Indeed, if that were true —
For Philip comes, one hand in mine, and one
Steadying   the   tremulous   pillars   of   the
        Church —
But no, no, no! Farewell. I am somewhat
        faint

With our long talk. Tho' Queen, I am not
    Queen
Of mine own heart, which every now and then
Beats me half dead: yet stay, this golden chain —
My father on a birthday gave it me,
And I have broken with my father — take
And wear it as memorial of a morning
Which found me full of foolish doubts, and
    leaves me
As hopeful.

            RENARD (*aside*).

        Whew — the folly of all follies
Is to be lovesick for a shadow. (*Aloud.*)
    Madam,
This chains me to your service, not with gold,
But dearest links of love. Farewell, and trust
    me,
Philip is yours.   [*Exit.*

           MARY.

        Mine — but not yet all mine.

        Enter USHER.

           USHER.

Your Council is in session, please your Majesty.

MARY.

Sir, let them sit.   I must have time to breathe.

No, say I come. (*Exit* USHER.)   I won by
    boldness once.

The Emperor counsell'd me to fly to Flanders.

I would not; but a hundred miles I rode,

Sent out my letters, call'd my friends together,

Struck home and won.

And when the Council would not crown me—
    thought

To bind me first by oaths I could not keep,

And keep with Christ and conscience—was it
    boldness

Or weakness that won there? when I, their
    Queen,

Cast myself down upon my knees before them,

And those hard men brake into woman-tears,

Even Gardiner, all amazed, and in that passion

Gave me my Crown.

Enter ALICE.

                 Girl, hast thou ever heard

Slanders against Prince Philip in our Court?

ALICE.

What slanders? I, your Grace; no, never.

MARY.

Nothing?

ALICE.

Never, your Grace.

MARY.

See that you neither hear them nor repeat!

ALICE (*aside*).

Good Lord! but I have heard a thousand such.
Ay, and repeated them as often — mum!
Why comes that old fox-Fleming back again?

Enter RENARD.

RENARD.

Madam, I scarce had left your Grace's presence
Before I chanced upon the messenger
Who brings that letter which we waited for —
The formal offer of Prince Philip's hand.
It craves an instant answer, Ay or No.

MARY.

An instant Ay or No! the Council sits.
Give it me quick.

ALICE (*stepping before her*).
>   Your Highness is all trembling.

MARY.

Make way.
>   [*Exit into the Council Chamber.*

ALICE.

>   O Master Renard, Master Renard,
If you have falsely painted your fine Prince,
Praised where you should have blamed him, I
>   pray God
No woman ever love you, Master Renard!
It breaks my heart to hear her moan at night
As tho' the nightmare never left her bed.

RENARD.

My pretty maiden, tell me, did you ever
Sigh for a beard?
>   ALICE.
>   That's not a pretty question.

RENARD.

Not prettily put?   I mean, my pretty maiden,
A pretty man for such a pretty maiden.

ALICE.

My Lord of Devon is a pretty man.
I hate him.   Well, but if I have, what then?

RENARD.

Then, pretty maiden, you should know that
          whether
A wind be warm or cold, it serves to fan
A kindled fire.
                    ALICE.

          According to the song.

His friends would praise him, I believed 'em,
     His foes would blame him, and I scorn'd 'em,
His friends — as Angels I received 'em,
     His foes — the Devil had suborn'd 'em.

RENARD.

Peace, pretty maiden.
I hear them stirring in the Council Chamber.
Lord Paget's ' Ay' is sure — who else? and yet,
They are all too much at odds to close at once
In one full-throated No!   Her Highness comes.

          Enter MARY.

ALICE.

How deathly pale! — a chair, your Highness.
                    [*Bringing one to the* QUEEN.

RENARD.

Madam,

The Council?

MARY.

Ay !   My Philip is all mine.
[*Sinks into chair, half fainting.*

ACT II.

SCENE I. — ALINGTON CASTLE.

SIR THOMAS WYATT.

I do not hear from Carew or the Duke
Of Suffolk, and till then I should not move.
The Duke hath gone to Leicester; Carew stirs
In Devon: that fine porcelain Courtenay,
Save that he fears he might be crack'd in using,
(I have known a semi-madman in my time
So fancy-ridden) should be in Devon too.

Enter WILLIAM.

News abroad, William?

WILLIAM.

None so new, Sir Thomas, and none so old,
Sir Thomas. No new news that Philip comes
to wed Mary, no old news that all men hate it.
Old Sir Thomas would have hated it. The bells
are ringing at Maidstone. Does n't your worship
hear?

SIR
THOMAS WYATT KNIGHT.

WYATT.

Ay, for the Saints are come to reign again.
Most like it is a Saint's-day.   There's no call
As yet for me; so in this pause, before
The mine be fired, it were a pious work
To string my father's sonnets, left about
Like loosely-scatter'd jewels, in fair order,
And head them with a lamer rhyme of mine,
To grace his memory.

WILLIAM.

Ay, why not, Sir Thomas?   He was a fine
courtier, he; Queen Anne loved him.   All the
women loved him.   I loved him, I was in Spain
with him.   I could n't eat in Spain, I could n't
sleep in Spain.   I hate Spain, Sir Thomas.

WYATT.

But thou could'st drink in Spain if I remember.

WILLIAM.

Sir Thomas, we may grant the wine.   Old Sir
Thomas always granted the wine.

WYATT.

Hand me the casket with my father's sonnets.

WILLIAM.

Ay — sonnets — a fine courtier of the old
Court, old Sir Thomas.　　　　　　　　[*Exit.*

WYATT.

Courtier of many courts, he loved the more
His own gray towers, plain life, and letter'd peace,
To read and rhyme in solitary fields,
The lark above, the nightingale below,
And answer them in song.　The sire begets
Not half his likeness in the son.　I fail
Where he was fullest: yet — to write it down.

　　　　　　　　　　　　　　[*He writes.*

Re-enter WILLIAM.

WILLIAM.

There *is* news, there *is* news, and no call
for sonnet-sorting now, nor for sonnet-making
either, but ten thousand men on Penenden Heath
all calling after your worship, and your worship's
name heard into Maidstone market, and your
worship the first man in Kent and Christendom,
for the Queen's down, and the world's up, and
your worship a-top of it.

WYATT.

Inverted Æsop — mountain out of mouse.
Say for ten thousand ten — and pot-house knaves,
Brain-dizzied with a draught of morning ale.

Enter ANTONY KNYVETT.

WILLIAM.

Here's Antony Knyvett.

KNYVETT.

    Look you, Master Wyatt,
Tear up that woman's work there.

WYATT.

       No; not these,
Dumb children of my father, that will speak
When I and thou and all rebellions lie
Dead bodies without voice. Song flies, you
  know,
For ages.
     KNYVETT.

   Tut, your sonnet's a flying ant,
Wing'd for a moment.

WYATT.

  Well, for mine own work,
   [*Tearing the paper.*
It lies there in six pieces at your feet;
For all that, I can carry it in my head.

KNYVETT.

If you can carry your head upon your shoulders.

WYATT.

I fear you come to carry it off my shoulders,
And sonnet-making's safer.

KNYVETT.

   Why, good Lord,
Write you as many sonnets as you will.
Ay, but not now; what, have you eyes, ears,
  brains?
This Philip and the black-faced swarms of Spain,
The hardest, cruellest people in the world,
Come locusting upon us, eat us up,
Confiscate lands, goods, money — Wyatt, Wyatt,
Wake, or the stout old island will become
A rotten limb of Spain.   They roar for you

On Penenden Heath, a thousand of them —
    more —
All arm'd, waiting a leader; there's no glory
Like his who saves his country: and you sit
Sing-songing here; but, if I'm any judge,
By God, you are as poor a poet, Wyatt,
As a good soldier.

WYATT.

          You as poor a critic
As an honest friend: you stroke me on one
    cheek,
Buffet the other.   Come, you bluster, Antony!
You know I know all this.   I must not move
Until I hear from Carew and the Duke.
I fear the mine is fired before the time.

KNYVETT (*showing a paper*).

But here's some Hebrew.   Faith, I half forgot
    it.
Look; can you make it English?   A strange
    youth
Suddenly thrust it on me, whisper'd, 'Wyatt,'
And whisking round a corner, show'd his back
Before I read his face.

WYATT.

　　　　Ha! Courtenay's cipher.
　　　　　　　　　　　　　[*Reads.*

'Sir Peter Carew fled to France: it is thought
the Duke will be taken. I am with you still;
but, for appearance sake, stay with the Queen.
Gardiner knows, but the Council are all at odds,
and the Queen hath no force for resistance.
Move, if you move, at once.'

Is Peter Carew fled? Is the Duke taken?
Down scabbard, and out sword! and let Rebellion
Roar till throne rock, and crown fall! No; not
　　　that;
But we will teach Queen Mary how to reign.
Who are those that shout below there?

KNYVETT.

　　　　　　　Why, some fifty
That follow'd me from Penenden Heath in hope
To hear you speak.

WYATT.

　　　　Open the window, Knyvett;
The mine is fired, and I will speak to them.

Men of Kent, England of England, you that
have kept your old customs upright, while all the
rest of England bowed theirs to the Norman,
the cause that hath brought us together is not
the cause of a county or a shire, but of this
England, in whose crown our Kent is the fairest
jewel.   Philip shall not wed Mary; and ye have
called me to be your leader.   I know Spain.   I
have been there with my father; I have seen them
in their own land; have marked the haughtiness
of their nobles, the cruelty of their priests.   If this
man marry our Queen, however the Council and
the Commons may fence round his power with
restriction, he will be King, King of England, my
masters; and the Queen, and the laws, and the
people, his slaves.   What? shall we have Spain
on the throne and in the parliament; Spain in
the pulpit and on the law-bench; Spain in all
the great offices of state; Spain in our ships, in
our forts, in our houses, in our beds?

CROWD.

No! no! no Spain!

William.

No Spain in our beds — that were worse than all. I have been there with old Sir Thomas, and the beds I know. I hate Spain.

A Peasant.

But, Sir Thomas, must we levy war against the Queen's Grace?

Wyatt.

No, my friend; war *for* the Queen's Grace — to save her from herself and Philip — war against Spain. And think not we shall be alone — thousands will flock to us. The Council, the Court itself, is on our side. The Lord Chancellor himself is on our side. The King of France is with us; the King of Denmark is with us; the world is with us — war against Spain! And if we move not now, yet it will be known that we have moved; and if Philip come to be King, O my God! The rope, the rack, the thumb-screw, the stake, the fire. If we move not now, Spain moves, bribes our nobles with her gold, and creeps, creeps snake-like about our legs till we cannot move at all; and ye know, my masters,

that wherever Spain hath ruled she hath wither'd
all beneath her.   Look at the New World —
a paradise made hell; the red man, that good
helpless creature, starved, maim'd, flogg'd,
flay'd, burn'd, boil'd, buried alive, worried by
dogs; and here, nearer home, the Netherlands,
Sicily, Naples, Lombardy.   I say no more —
only this, their lot is yours.   Forward to London
with me! forward to London!   If ye love your
liberties or your skins, forward to London!

CROWD.

Forward to London!   A Wyatt! a Wyatt!

WYATT.

But first to Rochester, to take the guns
From out the vessels lying in the river.
Then on.
A PEASANT.

Ay, but I fear we be too few, Sir Thomas.

WYATT.

Not many yet.   The world as yet, my friend,
Is not half-waked; but every parish tower
Shall clang and clash alarum as we pass,

And pour along the land, and swollen and fed
With indraughts and side-currents, in full force
Roll upon London.

CROWD.

A Wyatt! a Wyatt!   Forward!

KNYVETT.

Wyatt, shall we proclaim Elizabeth?

WYATT.

I 'll think upon it, Knyvett.

KNYVETT.

Or Lady Jane?

WYATT.

No, poor soul; no.
Ah, gray old castle of Alington, green field
Beside the brimming Medway, it may chance
That I shall never look upon you more.

KNYVETT.

Come, now, you 're sonnetting again.

WYATT.

Not I.

I 'll have my head set higher in the state;
Or — if the Lord God will it — on the stake.

[Exeunt.

SCENE II. — GUILDHALL.

SIR THOMAS WHITE (*The Lord Mayor*), LORD
WILLIAM HOWARD, SIR RALPH BAGENHALL,
ALDERMEN *and* CITIZENS.

WHITE.

I trust the Queen comes hither with her guards.

HOWARD.

Ay, all in arms.

[*Several of the citizens move hastily out of the
hall.*

Why do they hurry out there?

WHITE.

My Lord, cut out the rotten from your apple,
Your apple eats the better.   Let them go.
They go like those old Pharisees in John
Convicted by their conscience, arrant cowards,
Or tamperers with that treason out of Kent.
When will her Grace be here?

HOWARD.

In some few minutes.
She will address your guilds and companies.

I have striven in vain to raise a man for her.
But help her in this exigency, make
Your city loyal, and be the mightiest man
This day in England.

WHITE.

     I am Thomas White.
Few things have fail'd to which I set my will.
I do my most and best.

HOWARD.

     You know that after
The Captain Brett, who went with your train
  bands
To fight with Wyatt, had gone over to him
With all his men, the Queen in that distress
Sent Cornwallis and Hastings to the traitor,
Feigning to treat with him about her marriage —
Know too what Wyatt said.

WHITE.

     He 'd sooner be,
While this same marriage question was being
  argued,

Trusted than trust — the scoundrel — and de-
  manded
Possession of her person and the Tower.

HOWARD.
And four of her poor Council too, my Lord,
As hostages.
WHITE.
          I know it.   What do and say
Your Council at this hour?

HOWARD.
                    I will trust you.
We fling ourselves on you, my Lord.   The
  Council,
The Parliament as well, are troubled waters;
And yet like waters of the fen they know not
Which way to flow.   All hangs on her address
And upon you, Lord Mayor.

WHITE.
                How look'd the city
When now you past it?   Quiet?

HOWARD.
                    Like our Council,
Your city is divided.   As we past,

Some hail'd, some hiss'd us. There were citizens
Stood each before his shut-up booth, and look'd
As grim and grave as from a funeral.
And here a knot of ruffians all in rags,
With execrating execrable eyes,
Glared at the citizen. Here was a young mother,
Her face on flame, her red hair all blown back,
She shrilling ' Wyatt,' while the boy she held
Mimick'd and piped her ' Wyatt,' as red as she
In hair and cheek; and almost elbowing her,
So close they stood, another, mute as death,
And white as her own milk; her babe in arms
Had felt the faltering of his mother's heart,
And look'd as bloodless. Here a pious Catholic,
Mumbling and mixing up in his scared prayers
Heaven and earth's Maries; over his bow'd
        shoulder
Scowl'd that world-hated and world-hating
        beast,
A haggard Anabaptist. Many such groups.
The names of Wyatt, Elizabeth, Courtenay,
Nay, the Queen's right to reign — 'fore God, the
        rogues ! —
Were freely buzz'd among them. So I say

Your city is divided, and I fear
One scruple, this or that way, of success
Would turn it thither.   Wherefore now the
          Queen
In this low pulse and palsy of the state,
Bade me to tell you that she counts on you
And on myself as her two hands; on you,
In your own city, as her right, my Lord,
For you are loyal.

WHITE.
              Am I Thomas White?
One word before she comes.   Elizabeth —
Her name is much abused among these traitors.
Where is she?   She is loved by all of us.
I scarce have heart to mingle in this matter,
If she should be mishandled.

HOWARD.
              No; she shall not.
The Queen had written her word to come to
          court:
Methought I smelt out Renard in the letter,
And fearing for her, sent a secret missive,

Which told her to be sick.   Happily or not,
It found her sick indeed.

WHITE.

                    God send her well!
Here comes her Royal Grace.

Enter GUARDS, MARY, *and* GARDINER.   SIR
    THOMAS WHITE *leads her to a raised seat
    on the dais.*

WHITE.

I, the Lord Mayor, and these our companies
And guilds of London, gathered here, beseech
Your Highness to accept our lowliest thanks
For your most princely presence; and we pray
That we, your true and loyal citizens,
From your own royal lips, at once may know
The wherefore of this coming, and so learn
Your royal will, and do it. — I, Lord Mayor
Of London, and our guilds and companies.

MARY.

In mine own person am I come to you,
To tell you what indeed ye see and know,
How traitorously these rebels out of Kent

Have made strong head against ourselves and
    you.
They would not have me wed the Prince of
    Spain;
That was their pretext — so they spake at
    first —
But we sent divers of our Council to them,
And by their answers to the question ask'd,
It doth appear this marriage is the least
Of all their quarrel.
They have betrayed the treason of their hearts:
Seek to possess our person, hold our Tower,
Place and displace our councillors, and use
Both us and them according as they will.
Now what I am ye know right well — your
    Queen;
To whom, when I was wedded to the realm
And the realm's laws (the spousal ring whereof.
Not ever to be laid aside, I wear
Upon this finger), ye did promise full
Allegiance and obedience to the death.
Ye know my father was the rightful heir
Of England, and his right came down to me,
Corroborate by your acts of Parliament: .

And as ye were most loving unto him,
So doubtless will ye show yourselves to me.
Wherefore, ye will not brook that any one
Should seize our person, occupy our state,
More specially a traitor so presumptuous
As this same Wyatt, who hath tamper'd with
A public ignorance, and, under colour
Of such a cause as hath no colour, seeks
To bend the laws to his own will, and yield
Full scope to persons rascal and forlorn,
To make free spoil and havock of your goods.
Now, as your Prince, I say,
I, that was never mother, cannot tell
How mothers love their children; yet, methinks,
A prince as naturally may love his people
As these their children; and be sure your Queen
So loves you, and so loving, needs must deem
This love by you return'd as heartily;
And thro' this common knot and bond of love,
Doubt not they will be speedily overthrown.
As to this marriage, ye shall understand
We made thereto no treaty of ourselves,
And set no foot theretoward unadvised
Of all our Privy Council; furthermore,

This marriage had the assent of those to whom
The King, my father, did commit his trust;
Who not alone esteem'd it honourable,
But for the wealth and glory of our realm,
And all our loving subjects, most expedient.
As to myself,
I am not so set on wedlock as to choose
But where I list, nor yet so amorous
That I must needs be husbanded; I thank God,
I have lived a virgin, and I noway doubt
But that, with God's grace, I can live so still.
Yet if it might please God that I should leave
Some fruit of mine own body after me,
To be your king, ye would rejoice thereat,
And it would be your comfort, as I trust;
And truly, if I either thought or knew
This marriage should bring loss or danger to
        you,
My subjects, or impair in any way
This royal state of England, I would never
Consent thereto, nor marry while I live;
Moreover, if this marriage should not seem,
Before our own High Court of Parliament,
To be of rich advantage to our realm,

We will refrain, and not alone from this,
Likewise from any other, out of which
Looms the least chance of peril to our realm.
Wherefore be bold, and with your lawful Prince
Stand fast against our enemies and yours,
And fear them not. I fear them not. My Lord,
I leave Lord William Howard in your city,
To guard and keep you whole and safe from
        all
The spoil and sackage aim'd at by these rebels,
Who mouth and foam against the Prince of Spain.

VOICES.

Long live Queen Mary!
                    Down with Wyatt!
                              The Queen!
                WHITE.

Three voices from our guilds and companies!
You are shy and proud like Englishmen, my
        masters,
And will not trust your voices. Understand:
Your lawful Prince hath come to cast herself
On loyal hearts and bosoms, hoped to fall
Into the wide-spread arms of fealty,

And finds you statues.   Speak at once — and
    all!

For whom?

Our sovereign Lady by King Harry's will,

The Queen of England — or the Kentish Squire?

I know you loyal.   Speak! in the name of God!

The Queen of England or the rabble of Kent?

The reeking dungfork master of the mace!

Your havings wasted by the scythe and spade —

Your rights and charters hobnail'd into slush —

Your houses fired — your gutters bubbling
    blood —

ACCLAMATION.

No!   No!   The Queen! the Queen!

WHITE.

               Your Highness hears

This burst and bass of loyal harmony,

And how we each and all of us abhor

The venomous, bestial, devilish revolt

Of Thomas Wyatt.   Hear us now make oath

To raise your Highness thirty thousand men,

And arm and strike as with one hand, and brush

This Wyatt from our shoulders, like a flea

That might have leapt upon us unawares.
Swear with me, noble fellow-citizens, all,
With all your trades, and guilds, and companies.

Citizens.

We swear!

Mary.

We thank your Lordship and your loyal city.

[Exit Mary, *attended.*

White.

I trust this day, thro' God, I have saved the
crown.

First Alderman.

Ay, so my Lord of Pembroke in command
Of all her force be safe; but there are doubts.

Second Alderman.

I hear that Gardiner, coming with the Queen,
And meeting Pembroke, bent to his saddle-bow,
As if to win the man by flattering him.
Is he so safe to fight upon her side?

First Alderman.

If not, there's no man safe.

WHITE.

Yes, Thomas White.
I am safe enough; no man need flatter me.

SECOND ALDERMAN.

Nay, no man need; but did you mark our Queen?
The colour freely play'd into her face,
And the half sight which makes her look so
        stern
Seem'd thro' that dim dilated world of hers
To read our faces; I have never seen her
So queenly or so goodly.

WHITE.

Courage, sir,
That makes or man or woman look their good-
        liest.
Die like the torn fox dumb, but never whine
Like that poor heart, Northumberland, at the
        block.

BAGENHALL.

The man had children, and he whined for those.
Methinks most men are but poor-hearted, else
Should we so doat on courage, were it com-
        moner?

The Queen stands up, and speaks for her own
          self;
And all men cry, She is queenly, she is goodly.
Yet she's no goodlier; tho' my Lord Mayor
          here,
By his own rule, he hath been so bold to-day,
Should look more goodly than the rest of us.

WHITE.

Goodly?   I feel most goodly, heart and hand,
And strong to throw ten Wyatts and all Kent.
Ha! ha! sir; but you jest; I love it: a jest
In time of danger shows the pulses even.
Be merry! yet, Sir Ralph, you look but sad.
I dare avouch you'd stand up for yourself,
Tho' all the world should bay like winter wolves.

BAGENHALL.

Who knows? the man is proven by the hour.

WHITE.

The man should make the hour, not this the
          man;
And Thomas White will prove this Thomas
          Wyatt,

And he will prove an Iden to this Cade,
And he will play the Walworth to this Wat;
Come, sirs, we prate; hence all — gather your
    men —
Myself must bustle. Wyatt comes to South-
    wark;
I 'll have the drawbridge hewn into the Thames,
And see the citizens arm'd. Good day; good
    day.
                    [*Exit* WHITE.

BAGENHALL.

One of much outdoor bluster.

HOWARD.

                For all that,
Most honest, brave, and skilful; and his
    wealth
A fountain of perennial alms — his fault
So thoroughly to believe in his own self.

BAGENHALL.

Yet thoroughly to believe in one's own self,
So one's own self be thorough, were to do
Great things, my Lord.

HOWARD.

It may be.

BAGENHALL.

I have heard
One of your Council fleer and jeer at him.

HOWARD.

The nursery-cocker'd child will jeer at aught
That may seem strange beyond his nursery.
The statesman that shall jeer and fleer at men,
Makes enemies for himself and for his king;
And if he jeer, not seeing the true man
Behind his folly, he is thrice the fool;
And if he see the man and still will jeer,
He is child and fool, and traitor to the State.
Who is he? let me shun him.

BAGENHALL.

Nay, my Lord,
He is damn'd enough already.

HOWARD.

I must set
The guard at Ludgate. Fare you well, Sir
Ralph.

BAGENHALL.

'Who knows?' I am for England.   But who
    knows,
That knows the Queen, the Spaniard, and the
    Pope,
Whether I be for Wyatt, or the Queen?

                                    [*Exeunt.*

SCENE III. — LONDON BRIDGE.

Enter SIR THOMAS WYATT *and* BRETT.

WYATT.

Brett, when the Duke of Norfolk moved against
    us
Thou criedst 'A Wyatt!' and flying to our side
Left his all bare, for which I love thee, Brett.
Have for thine asking aught that I can give,
For thro' thine help we are come to London
    Bridge;
But how to cross it balks me.   I fear we cannot.

BRETT.

Nay, hardly, save by boat, swimming, or wings.

WYATT.

Last night I climb'd into the gate-house, Brett,
And scared the gray old porter and his wife.
And then I crept along the gloom and saw
They had hewn the drawbridge down into the
    river.
It roll'd as black as death; and that same tide
Which, coming with our coming, seem'd to
    smile`
And sparkle like our fortune as thou saidest,
Ran sunless down, and moan'd against the piers.
But o'er the chasm I saw Lord William Howard
By torchlight, and his guard; four guns gaped
    at me,
Black, silent mouths: had Howard spied me
    there
And made them speak, as well he might have
    done,
Their voice had left me none to tell you this.
What shall we do?

BRETT.

    On somehow. To go back
Were to lose all.

Wyatt.

On over London Bridge
We cannot: stay we cannot; there is ordnance
On the White Tower and on the Devil's Tower,
And pointed full at Southwark; we must round
By Kingston Bridge.

Brett.

Ten miles about.

Wyatt.

Even so.

But I have notice from our partisans
Within the city that they will stand by us
If Ludgate can be reach'd by dawn to-morrow.

Enter one of Wyatt's *men.*

Man.

Sir Thomas, I've found this paper; pray your
worship read it; I know not my letters; the old
priests taught me nothing.

Wyatt (*reads*).

'Whosoever will apprehend the traitor Thomas
Wyatt shall have a hundred pounds for reward.'

MAN.

Is that it?   That's a big lot of money.

WYATT.

Ay, ay, my friend; not read it? 't is not written
Half plain enough.   Give me a piece of paper!
> [*Writes* 'THOMAS WYATT' *large.*

There, any man can read that.
> [*Sticks it in his cap.*

BRETT.
> But that's foolhardy.

WYATT.

No! boldness, which will give my followers boldness.

Enter MAN *with a prisoner.*

MAN.

We found him, your worship, a-plundering o'
Bishop Winchester's house; he says he's a poor
gentleman.

WYATT.

Gentleman! a thief!   Go hang him.   Shall we
make
Those that we come to serve our sharpest foes?

BRETT.

Sir Thomas —

WYATT.

Hang him, I say.

BRETT.

Wyatt, but now you promised me a boon.

WYATT.

Ay, and I warrant this fine fellow's life.

BRETT.

Even so; he was my neighbour once in Kent.
He's poor enough, has drunk and gambled out
All that he had, and gentleman he was.
We have been glad together; let him live.

WYATT.

He has gambled for his life and lost, he hangs.
No, no, my word's my word.   Take thy poor
          gentleman!
Gamble thyself at once out of my sight,
Or I will dig thee with my dagger.   Away!
Women and children!

Enter a Crowd *of* Women *and* Children.

First Woman.

O Sir Thomas, Sir Thomas, pray you go
away, Sir Thomas, or you 'll make the White
Tower a black 'un for us this blessed day.   He 'll
be the death on us; and you 'll set the Divil's
Tower a-spitting, and he 'll smash all our bits o'
things worse than Philip o' Spain.

Second Woman.

Don't ye now go to think that we be for Philip
o' Spain.

Third Woman.

No, we know that ye be come to kill the
Queen, and we 'll pray for you all on our bended
knees.   But o' God's mercy don't ye kill the
Queen here, Sir Thomas; look ye, here 's little
Dickon, and little Robin, and little Jenny —
though she 's but a side-cousin — and all on our
knees, we pray you to kill the Queen further off,
Sir Thomas.

Wyatt.

My friends, I have not come to kill the Queen
Or here or there: I come to save you all,
And I 'll go further off.

CROWD.

Thanks, Sir Thomas, we be beholden to you,
and we'll pray for you on our bended knees till
our lives' end.

WYATT.

Be happy, I am your friend. To Kingston,
      forward!   [*Exeunt.*

SCENE IV. — ROOM IN THE GATE-HOUSE OF
WESTMINSTER PALACE.

MARY, ALICE, GARDINER, RENARD, LADIES.

GARDINER.

Their cry is, Philip never shall be king.

MARY.

Lord Pembroke in command of all our force
Will front their cry and shatter them into dust.

ALICE.

Was not Lord Pembroke with Northumberland?
O madam, if this Pembroke should be false?

MARY.

No, girl; most brave and loyal, brave and loyal.
His breaking with Northumberland broke North-
    umberland.
At the park gate he hovers with our guards.
These Kentish ploughmen cannot break the
    guards.

Enter MESSENGER.

MESSENGER.

Wyatt, your Grace, hath broken thro' the guards
And gone to Ludgate.

GARDINER.

             Madam, I much fear
That all is lost; but we can save your Grace.
The river still is free. I do beseech you,
There yet is time, take boat and pass to Windsor.

MARY.

I pass to Windsor and I lose my crown.

GARDINER.

Pass, then, I pray your Highness, to the Tower.

MARY.

I shall but be their prisoner in the Tower.

CRIES WITHOUT.

The traitor! treason! Pembroke!

LADIES.

Treason! treason!

MARY.

Peace.

False to Northumberland, is he false to me?
Bear witness, Renard, that I live and die
The true and faithful bride of Philip — A sound
Of feet and voices thickening hither — blows —
Hark, there is battle at the palace gates,
And I will out upon the gallery.

LADIES.

No, no, your Grace; see there the arrows flying.

MARY.

I am Harry's daughter, Tudor, and not Fear.

[*Goes out on the gallery.*

The guards are all driven in, skulk into corners
Like rabbits to their holes.   A gracious guard

Truly; shame on them! they have shut the
　　gates!

Enter SIR ROBERT SOUTHWELL.

SOUTHWELL.

The porter, please your Grace, hath shut the
　　gates
On friend and foe.　Your gentlemen-at-arms,
If this be not your Grace's order, cry
To have the gates set wide again, and they
With their good battle-axes will do you right
Against all traitors.

MARY.

They are the flower of England; set the gates
　　wide.
　　　　　　　[*Exit* SOUTHWELL.

Enter COURTENAY.

COURTENAY.

All lost, all lost, all yielded!　A barge, a barge!
The Queen must to the Tower.

MARY.

　　　　　Whence come you, sir?

Courtenay.

From Charing Cross; the rebels broke us there,
And I sped hither with what haste I might
To save my royal cousin.

Mary.

                        Where is Pembroke?

Courtenay.

I left him somewhere in the thick of it.

Mary.

Left him and fled; and thou that would'st be
        King,
And hast nor heart nor honour!   I myself
Will down into the battle and there bide
The upshot of my quarrel, or die with those
That are no cowards and no Courtenays.

Courtenay.

I do not love your Grace should call me coward.

Enter another Messenger.

Messenger.

Over, your Grace, all crush'd; the brave Lord
        William

Thrust him from Ludgate, and the traitor flying
To Temple Bar, there by Sir Maurice Berkeley
Was taken prisoner.

MARY.

To the Tower with *him!*

MESSENGER.

'T is said he told Sir Maurice there was one
Cognisant of this, and party thereunto,
My Lord of Devon.

MARY.

To the Tower with *him!*

COURTENAY.

O la, the Tower, the Tower, always the Tower,
I shall grow into it — I shall be the Tower.

MARY.

Your Lordship may not have so long to wait.
Remove him!

COURTENAY.

La, to whistle out my life,
And carve my coat upon the walls again!

[*Exit* COURTENAY, *guarded.*

MESSENGER.

Also this Wyatt did confess the Princess
Cognisant thereof, and party thereunto.

MARY.

What? whom — whom did you say?

MESSENGER.

Elizabeth,
Your royal sister.

MARY.

To the Tower with *her!*
My foes are at my feet, and I am Queen.

[GARDINER *and her* LADIES *kneel to her.*

GARDINER (*rising*).

There let them lie, your footstool! (*Aside.*)
    Can I strike
Elizabeth? — not now and save the life
Of Devon: if I save him, he and his
Are bound to me — may strike hereafter.
    (*Aloud.*) Madam,
What Wyatt said, or what they said he said,
Cries of the moment and the street —

MARY.

He said it.

GARDINER.

Your courts of justice will determine that.

RENARD (*advancing*).

I trust by this your Highness will allow
Some spice of wisdom in my telling you,
When last we talk'd, that Philip would not come
Till Guildford Dudley and the Duke of Suffolk
And Lady Jane had left us.

MARY.

They shall die.

RENARD.

And your so loving sister?

MARY.

She shall die.
My foes are at my feet, and Philip King.

[*Exeunt.*

ACT III.

SCENE I. — The Conduit in Gracechurch,

Painted with the Nine Worthies, among them King Henry VIII. holding a book, on it inscribed 'Verbum Dei.'

Enter Sir Ralph Bagenhall *and* Sir Thomas Stafford.

Bagenhall.

A hundred here and hundreds hang'd in Kent.
The tigress had unsheath'd her nails at last,
And Renard and the Chancellor sharpen'd them.
In every London street a gibbet stood.
They are down to-day.   Here by this house was
    one ;
The traitor husband dangled at the door,
And when the traitor wife came out for bread
To still the petty treason therewithin,
Her cap would brush his heels.

STAFFORD.

It is Sir Ralph,
And muttering to himself as heretofore.
Sir, see you aught up yonder?

BAGENHALL.

I miss something.
The tree that only bears dead fruit is gone.

STAFFORD.

What tree, sir?

BAGENHALL.

Well, the tree in Virgil, sir,
That bears not its own apples.

STAFFORD.

What! the gallows?

BAGENHALL.

Sir, this dead fruit was ripening overmuch,
And had to be removed lest living Spain
Should sicken at dead England.

STAFFORD.

Not so dead
But that a shock may rouse her.

BAGENHALL.

                                        I believe

Sir Thomas Stafford?

STAFFORD.

                              I am ill disguised.

BAGENHALL.

Well, are you not in peril here?

STAFFORD.

                                        I think so.

I came to feel the pulse of England, whether
It beats hard at this marriage.   Did you see it?

BAGENHALL.

Stafford, I am a sad man and a serious.
Far liefer had I in my country hall
Been reading some old book, with mine old
        hound
Couch'd at my hearth, and mine old flask of
        wine
Beside me, than have seen it: yet I saw it.

STAFFORD.

Good, was it splendid?

BAGENHALL.

          Ay, if Dukes, and Earls,
And Counts, and sixty Spanish cavaliers,
Some six or seven Bishops, diamonds, pearls,
That royal commonplace too, cloth of gold,
Could make it so.

STAFFORD.

        And what was Mary's dress?

BAGENHALL.

Good faith, I was too sorry for the woman
To mark the dress.   She wore red shoes!

STAFFORD.

              Red shoes!

BAGENHALL.

Scarlet, as if her feet were wash'd in blood,
As if she had waded in it.

STAFFORD.

            Were your eyes
So bashful that you look'd no higher?

BAGENHALL.

             A diamond,
And Philip's gift, as proof of Philip's love,

Who hath not any for any, — tho' a true one,
Blazed false upon her heart.

STAFFORD.
              But this proud Prince —

BAGENHALL.
Nay, he is King, you know, the King of Naples
The father ceded Naples that the son,
Being a King, might wed a Queen — Oh, he
Flamed in brocade — white satin his trunk-hose,
Inwrought with silver, — on his neck a collar,
Gold, thick with diamonds; hanging down from
      this
The Golden Fleece — and round his knee, mis-
      placed,
Our English Garter, studded with great emeralds,
Rubies, I know not what. Have you had enough
Of all this gear?
                STAFFORD.
              Ay, since you hate the telling it.
How look'd the Queen?

BAGENHALL.
                No fairer for her jewels.
And I could see that as the new-made couple
VOL. XI. — 8

Came from the Minster, moving side by side
Beneath one canopy, ever and anon
She cast on him a vassal smile of love,
Which Philip with a glance of some distaste,
Or so methought, return'd. I may be wrong,
  sir.
This marriage will not hold.

STAFFORD.

      I think with you.
The King of France will help to break it.

BAGENHALL.

        France!
We once had half of France, and hurl'd our
  battles
Into the heart of Spain; but England now
Is but a ball chuck'd between France and Spain,
His in whose hand she drops; Harry of Boling-
  broke
Had holpen Richard's tottering throne to stand,
Could Harry have foreseen that all our nobles
Would perish on the civil slaughter-field,
And leave the people naked to the crown,
And the crown naked to the people; the crown

Female, too!   Sir, no woman's regimen
Can save us.   We are fallen, and, as I think,
Never to rise again.

STAFFORD.

> You are too black-blooded.
I'd make a move myself to hinder that:
I know some lusty fellows there in France.

BAGENHALL.

You would but make us weaker, Thomas Stafford.
Wyatt was a good soldier, yet he fail'd,
And strengthen'd Philip.

STAFFORD.

> Did not his last breath
Clear Courtenay and the Princess from the charge
Of being his co-rebels?

BAGENHALL.

> Ay, but then
What such a one as Wyatt says is nothing:
We have no men among us.   The new Lords
Are quieted with their sop of Abbey-lands,
And even before the Queen's face Gardiner buys
        them

With Philip's gold. All greed, no faith, no
    courage!
Why, even the haughty prince, Northumberland,
The leader of our Reformation, knelt
And blubber'd like a lad, and on the scaffold
Recanted, and resold himself to Rome.

STAFFORD.

I swear you do your country wrong, Sir Ralph.
I know a set of exiles over there,
Dare-devils, that would eat fire and spit it out
At Philip's beard: they pillage Spain already.
The French King winks at it. An hour will
    come
When they will sweep her from the seas. No
    men?
Did not Lord Suffolk die like a true man?
Is not Lord William Howard a true man?
Yea, you yourself, altho' you are black-blooded:
And I, by God, believe myself a man.
Ay, even in the church there is a man —
Cranmer.
Fly would he not, when all men bade him fly.
And what a letter he wrote against the Pope!
There's a brave man, if any.

BAGENHALL.
                    Ay ; if it hold.

CROWD (*coming on*).
God save their Graces!

STAFFORD.
                    Bagenhall, I see
The Tudor green and white. (*Trumpets.*) They
    are coming now.
And here 's a crowd as thick as herring-shoals.

BAGENHALL.
Be limpets to this pillar, or we are torn
Down the strong wave of brawlers.

CROWD.
God save their Graces!

*Procession of Trumpeters, Javelinmen, etc. ; then
    Spanish and Flemish Nobles intermingled.*

STAFFORD.
Worth seeing, Bagenhall!   These black dog-
    Dons
Garb themselves bravely.   Who 's the long-face
    there,
Looks very Spain of very Spain?

BAGENHALL.
                              The Duke
Of Alva, an iron soldier.

STAFFORD.
                              And the Dutchman,
Now laughing at some jest?

BAGENHALL.
                              William of Orange,
William the Silent.

STAFFORD.
                    Why do they call him so?

BAGENHALL.
He keeps, they say, some secret that may cost
Philip his life.
                    STAFFORD.
                    But then he looks so merry.

BAGENHALL.
I cannot tell you why they call him so.

The KING *and* QUEEN *pass, attended by Peers of
the Realm, Officers of State, etc. Cannon shot
off.*

CROWD.

Philip and Mary, Philip and Mary!

Long live the King and Queen, Philip and Mary!

STAFFORD.

They smile as if content with one another.

BAGENHALL.

A smile abroad is oft a scowl at home.

[KING *and* QUEEN *pass on.   Procession.*

FIRST CITIZEN.

I thought this Philip had been one of those black devils of Spain, but he hath a yellow beard.

SECOND CITIZEN.

Not red like Iscariot's.

FIRST CITIZEN.

Like a carrot's, as thou say'st, and English carrot's better than Spanish licorice; but I thought he was a beast.

THIRD CITIZEN.

Certain I had heard that every Spaniard carries a tail like a devil under his trunk-hose.

Tailor.

Ay, but see what trunk-hoses! Lord! they
be fine; I never stitch'd none such. They make
amends for the tails.

Fourth Citizen.

Tut! every Spanish priest will tell you that all
English heretics have tails.

Fifth Citizen.

Death and the Devil — if he find I have
one —

Fourth Citizen.

Lo! thou hast call'd them up! here they come
— a pale horse for Death, and Gardiner for the
Devil.

Enter Gardiner (*turning back from the procession*).

Gardiner.

Knave, wilt thou wear thy cap before the Queen?

Man.

My Lord, I stand so squeezed among the crowd
I cannot lift my hands unto my head.

GARDINER.

Knock off his cap there, some of you about him!
See there be others that can use their hands.
Thou art one of Wyatt's men?

MAN.
No, my Lord, no.

GARDINER.

Thy name, thou knave?

MAN.
I am nobody, my Lord.

GARDINER (*shouting*).

God's passion! knave, thy name?

MAN.
I have ears to hear.

GARDINER.

Ay, rascal, if I leave thee ears to hear.
Find out his name and bring it me (*to Attendant*).

ATTENDANT.
Ay, my Lord.

GARDINER.

Knave, thou shalt lose thine ears and find thy
tongue,

And shalt be thankful if I leave thee that.

[*Coming before the Conduit.*

The conduit painted — the Nine Worthies — ay!
But then what's here?   King Harry with a
   scroll.
Ha — Verbum Dei — verbum — Word of God!
God's passion! do you know the knave that
   painted it?

ATTENDANT.

I do, my Lord.

GARDINER.

      Tell him to paint it out,
And put some fresh device in lieu of it —
A pair of gloves, a pair of gloves, sir; ha?
There is no heresy there.

ATTENDANT.

      I will, my Lord;
The man shall paint a pair of gloves.   I am sure
(Knowing the man) he wrought it ignorantly,
And not from any malice.

GARDINER.

      Word of God
In English! over this the brainless loons

That cannot spell Esaias from Saint Paul,
Make themselves drunk and mad, fly out and
      flare
Into rebellions.   I 'll have their Bibles burnt.
The Bible is the priest's.   Ay! fellow, what!
Stand staring at me! shout, you gaping rogue!

MAN.

I have, my Lord, shouted till I am hoarse.

GARDINER.

What hast thou shouted, knave?

MAN.

          Long live Queen Mary!

GARDINER.

Knave, there be two.   There be both King and
      Queen,
Philip and Mary.   Shout!

MAN.

          Nay, but, my Lord,
The Queen comes first, Mary and Philip.

GARDINER.

          Shout, then,
Mary and Philip!

MAN.

Mary and Philip!

GARDINER.

Now,

Thou hast shouted for thy pleasure, shout for
    mine!

Philip and Mary!

MAN.

Must it be so, my Lord?

GARDINER.

Ay, knave.

MAN.

Philip and Mary!

GARDINER.

I distrust thee.

Thine is a half voice and a lean assent.

What is thy name?

MAN.

Sanders.

GARDINER.

What else?

MAN.

Zerubbabel.

GARDINER.

Where dost thou live?

MAN.

In Cornhill.

GARDINER.

Where, knave, where?

MAN.

Sign of the Talbot.

GARDINER.

Come to me to-morrow. —
Rascal! — this land is like a hill of fire,
One crater opens when another shuts.
But so I get the laws against the heretic,
Spite of Lord Paget and Lord William Howard,
And others of our Parliament, revived,
I will show fire on my side — stake and fire —
Sharp work and short. The knaves are easily
    cow'd.
Follow their Majesties.

                    [*Exit. The crowd following.*

BAGENHALL.

                    As proud as Becket.

STAFFORD.

You would not have him murder'd as Becket
    was?

BAGENHALL.

No — murder fathers murder: but I say
There is no man — there was one woman with
    us —
It was a sin to love her married, dead
I cannot choose but love her.

STAFFORD.

               Lady Jane?

CROWD (*going off*).

God save their Graces!

STAFFORD.

            Did you see her die?

BAGENHALL.

No, no; her innocent blood had blinded me.
You call me too black-blooded — true enough,
Her dark, dead blood is in my heart with mine.
If ever I cry out against the Pope
Her dark, dead blood that ever moves with mine
Will stir the living tongue and make the cry.

STAFFORD.

Yet doubtless you can tell me how she died?

BAGENHALL.

Seventeen — and knew eight languages — in
    music
Peerless — her needle perfect, and her learning
Beyond the churchmen; yet so meek, so modest,
So wife-like humble to the trivial boy
Mismatch'd with her for policy! I have heard
She would not take a last farewell of him;
She fear'd it might unman him for his end.
She could not be unmann'd — no, nor out-
    woman'd —
Seventeen — a rose of grace!
Girl never breathed to rival such a rose;
Rose never blew that equall'd such a bud.

STAFFORD.

Pray you go on.

BAGENHALL.

      She came upon the scaffold,
And said she was condemn'd to die for treason;

She had but follow'd the device of those
Her nearest kin: she thought they knew the
    laws.
But for herself, she knew but little law,
And nothing of the titles to the crown;
She had no desire for that, and wrung her hands,
And trusted God would save her thro' the blood
Of Jesus Christ alone.

STAFFORD.

Pray you go on.

BAGENHALL.

Then knelt and said the Miserere Mei —
But all in English, mark you; rose again,
And, when the headsman pray'd to be forgiven,
Said, 'You will give me my true crown at last,
But do it quickly;' then all wept but she,
Who changed not colour when she saw the block,
But ask'd him, childlike, 'Will you take it off
Before I lay me down?' 'No, madam,' he said,
Gasping; and when her innocent eyes were
    bound,
She, with her poor blind hands feeling — 'Where
    is it?

Where is it?' — You must fancy that which
   follow'd,
If you have heart to do it!

CROWD (*in the distance*).
                    God save their Graces!

STAFFORD.

Their Graces, our disgraces! God confound
   them!
Why, she's grown bloodier! when I last was
   here,
This was against her conscience — would be
   murder!

BAGENHALL.

The 'Thou shalt do no murder,' which God's
   hand
Wrote on her conscience, Mary rubb'd out
   pale —
She could not make it white — and over that,
Traced in the blackest text of Hell — 'Thou
   shalt!'
And sign'd it — Mary!

STAFFORD.

          Philip and the Pope

Must have sign'd too. I hear this Legate's
     coming

To bring us absolution from the Pope.

The Lords and Commons will bow down before
     him—

You are of the house? what will you do, Sir
     Ralph?

BAGENHALL.

And why should I be bolder than the rest,

Or honester than all?

STAFFORD.

          But, sir, if I—

And over-sea they say this state of yours

Hath no more mortice than a tower of cards;

And that a puff would do it — then if I

And others made that move I touched upon,

Back'd by the power of France, and landing
     here,

Came with a sudden splendour, shout, and show,

And dazzled men and deafen'd by some bright

Loud venture, and the people so unquiet —

And I the race of murder'd Buckingham —
Not for myself, but for the kingdom — Sir,
I trust that you would fight along with us.

BAGENHALL.

No; you would fling your lives into the gulf.

STAFFORD.

But if this Philip, as he's like to do,
Left Mary a wife-widow here alone,
Set up a viceroy, sent his myriads hither
To seize upon the forts and fleet, and make us
A Spanish province; would you not fight then?

BAGENHALL.

I think I should fight then.

STAFFORD.

                                        I am sure of it.
Hist! there's the face coming on here of one
Who knows me. I must leave you. Fare you
        well,
You'll hear of me again.

BAGENHALL.

                                Upon the scaffold.
                                        [*Exeunt.*

SCENE II. — ROOM IN WHITEHALL PALACE.

MARY.   *Enter* PHILIP *and* CARDINAL POLE.

POLE.

Ave Maria, gratia plena, benedicta tu in muli-
    eribus!

MARY.

Loyal and royal cousin, humblest thanks.
Had you a pleasant voyage up the river?

POLE.

We had your royal barge, and that same chair,
Or rather throne of purple, on the deck.
Our silver cross sparkled before the prow,
The ripples twinkled at their diamond-dance,
The boats that follow'd were as glowing-gay
As regal gardens, and your flocks of swans
As fair and white as angels; and your shores
Wore in mine eyes the green of Paradise.
My foreign friends, who dream'd us blanketed
In ever-closing fog, were much amazed
To find as fair a sun as might have flash'd
Upon their lake of Garda fire the Thames;

Our voyage by sea was all but miracle;
And here the river flowing from the sea,
Not toward it (for they thought not of our tides),
Seem'd as a happy miracle to make glide —
In quiet — home your banish'd countryman.

MARY.

We heard that you were sick in Flanders, cousin.

POLE.

A dizziness.

MARY.

And how came you round again?

POLE.

The scarlet thread of Rahab saved her life;
And mine, a little letting of the blood.

MARY.

Well? now?

POLE.

Ay, cousin, as the heathen giant
Had but to touch the ground, his force return'd —
Thus, after twenty years of banishment,
Feeling my native land beneath my foot,
I said thereto: 'Ah, native land of mine,
Thou art much beholden to this foot of mine,

That hastes with full commission from the Pope
To absolve thee from thy guilt of heresy.
Thou hast disgraced me and attainted me,
And mark'd me even as Cain, and I return
As Peter, but to bless thee: make me well.'
Methinks the good land heard me, for to-day
My heart beats twenty, when I see you, cousin.
Ah, gentle cousin, since your Herod's death,
How oft hath Peter knock'd at Mary's gate!
And Mary would have risen and let him in,
But, Mary, there were those within the house
Who would not have it.

MARY.

    True, good cousin Pole;
And there were also those without the house
Who would not have it.

POLE.

    I believe so, cousin.
State-policy and church-policy are conjoint,
But Janus-faces looking diverse ways.
I fear the Emperor much misvalued me.
But all is well; 'twas even the will of God,

Who, waiting till the time had ripen'd, now
Makes me His mouth of holy greeting.   'Hail,
Daughter of God, and saver of the faith.
Sit benedictus fructus ventris tui ! '

MARY.

Ah, heaven !

POLE.

Unwell, your Grace?

MARY.

No, cousin, happy —
Happy to see you ; never yet so happy
Since I was crown'd.

POLE.

Sweet cousin, you forget
That long low minster where you gave your
        hand
To this great Catholic King.

PHILIP.

Well said, Lord Legate.

MARY.

Nay, not well said ; I thought of you, my liege,
Even as I spoke.

PHILIP.

         Ay, Madam; my Lord Paget
Waits to present our Council to the Legate.
Sit down here, all; Madam, between us you.

POLE.

Lo, now you are enclosed with boards of cedar,
Our little sister of the Song of Songs!
You are doubly fenced and shielded sitting here
Between the two most high-set thrones on earth,
The Emperor's highness happily symboll'd by
The King your husband, the Pope's holiness
By mine own self.

MARY.

         True, cousin, I am happy.
When will you that we summon both our houses
To take this absolution from your lips,
And be re-gather'd to the Papal fold?

POLE.

In Britain's calendar the brightest day
Beheld our rough forefathers break their gods,
And clasp the faith in Christ; but after that
Might not Saint Andrew's be her happiest day?

MARY.

Then these shall meet upon Saint Andrew's Day.

Enter PAGET, *who presents the Council.   Dumb
show.*

POLE.

I am an old man wearied with my journey,
Even with my joy.   Permit me to withdraw.
To Lambeth?

PHILIP.

Ay, Lambeth has ousted Cranmer.
It was not meet the heretic swine should live
In Lambeth.

MARY.

There or anywhere, or at all.

PHILIP.

We have had it swept and garnish'd after him.

POLE.

Not for the seven devils to enter in?

PHILIP.

No, for we trust they parted in the swine.

POLE.

True, and I am the Angel of the Pope.
Farewell, your Graces.

PHILIP.

          Nay, not here — to me;
I will go with you to the waterside.

POLE.

Not be my Charon to the counter side?

PHILIP.

No, my Lord Legate, the Lord Chancellor goes.

POLE.

And unto no dead world; but Lambeth Palace,
Henceforth a centre of the living faith.
          [*Exeunt* PHILIP, POLE, PAGET, *etc.*

Manet MARY.

MARY.

He hath awaked! he hath awaked!
He stirs within the darkness!
O Philip, husband! now thy love to mine
Will cling more close, and those bleak manners
      thaw,
That make me shamed and tongue-tied in my
      love.
The second Prince of Peace —

CARDINAL POLE.

The great unborn defender of the Faith,
Who will avenge me of mine enemies —
He comes, and my star rises.
The stormy Wyatts and Northumberlands,
The proud ambitions of Elizabeth,
And all her fieriest partisans — are pale
Before my star!
The light of this new learning wanes and dies:
The ghosts of Luther and Zuinglius fade
Into the deathless hell which is their doom
Before my star!
His sceptre shall go forth from Ind to Ind!
His sword shall hew the heretic peoples down!
His faith shall clothe the world that will be his,
Like universal air and sunshine!   Open,
Ye everlasting gates!   The King is here! —
My star, my son!

Enter PHILIP, DUKE OF ALVA, *etc.*

Oh, Philip, come with me!
Good news have I to tell you, news to make
Both of us happy — ay, the kingdom too.
Nay come with me — one moment!

PHILIP (*to* ALVA).

More than that:
There was one here of late — William the Silent
They call him — he is free enough in talk,
But tells me nothing.   You will be, we trust,
Sometime the viceroy of those provinces —
He must deserve his surname better.

ALVA.

Ay, sir;

Inherit the Great Silence.

PHILIP.

True; the provinces
Are hard to rule and must be hardly ruled;
Most fruitful, yet, indeed, an empty rind,
All hollow'd out with stinging heresies;
And for their heresies, Alva, they will fight;
You must break them or they break you.

ALVA (*proudly*).

The first.

PHILIP.

Good!
Well, Madam, this new happiness of mine?

[*Exeunt.*

Enter THREE PAGES.

FIRST PAGE.

News, mates! a miracle, a miracle! news!
The bells must ring; Te Deums must be sung;
The Queen hath felt the motion of her babe!

SECOND PAGE.

Ay; but see here!

FIRST PAGE.

See what?

SECOND PAGE.

This paper, Dickon.
I found it fluttering at the palace gates: —
'The Queen of England is delivered of a dead
dog!'

THIRD PAGE.

These are the things that madden her. Fie
upon it!

FIRST PAGE.

Ay; but I hear she hath a dropsy, lad,
Or a high-dropsy, as the doctors call it.

THIRD PAGE.

Fie on her dropsy, so she have a dropsy!
I know that she was ever sweet to me.

FIRST PAGE.

For thou and thine are Roman to the core.

THIRD PAGE.

So thou and thine must be.   Take heed!

FIRST PAGE.

Not I;

And whether this flash of news be false or true,
So the wine run, and there be revelry,
Content am I.   Let all the steeples clash,
Till the sun dance, as upon Easter Day.

[Exeunt.

SCENE III. — GREAT HALL IN WHITEHALL.

*At the far end a dais.   On this three chairs, two
    under one canopy for* MARY *and* PHILIP, *another
    on the right of these for* POLE.   *Under the dais
    on* POLE'S *side, ranged along the wall, sit all
    the Spiritual Peers, and along the wall opposite
    all the Temporal.   The Commons on cross
    benches in front, a line of approach to the dais
    between them.   In the foreground,* SIR RALPH
    BAGENHALL *and other* MEMBERS *of the* COM-
    MONS.

FIRST MEMBER.

Saint Andrew's Day; sit close, sit close, we are
     friends.
Is reconciled the word? the Pope again?
It must be thus; and yet, cocksbody! how strange
That Gardiner, once so one with all of us
Against this foreign marriage, should have yielded
So utterly! — strange! but stranger still that he,
So fierce against the headship of the Pope,
Should play the second actor in this pageant
That brings him in; such a cameleon he!

SECOND MEMBER.

This Gardiner turn'd his coat in Henry's time;
The serpent that hath slough'd will slough again.

THIRD MEMBER.

Tut, then we all are serpents.

SECOND MEMBER.

               Speak for yourself.

THIRD MEMBER.

Ay, and for Gardiner! being English citizen,
How should he bear a bridegroom out of Spain?

The Queen would have him! being English
    churchman,
How should he bear the headship of the Pope?
The Queen would have it! Statesmen that are
    wise
Shape a necessity, as a sculptor clay,
To their own model.

SECOND MEMBER.

              Statesmen that are wise
Take truth herself for model. What say you?
          [*To* SIR RALPH BAGENHALL.

BAGENHALL.

We talk and talk.

FIRST MEMBER.

            Ay, and what use to talk?
Philip's no sudden alien — the Queen's husband,
He's here, and King, or will be — yet, cocksbody!
So hated here! I watch'd a hive of late;
My seven-years' friend was with me, my young
    boy;
Out crept a wasp, with half the swarm behind.
'Philip!' says he. I had to cuff the rogue
For infant treason.

THIRD MEMBER.

                    But they say that bees,
If any creeping life invade their hive
Too gross to be thrust out, will build him round,
And bind him in from harming of their combs.
And Philip by these articles is bound
From stirring hand or foot to wrong the realm.

SECOND MEMBER.

By bonds of beeswax, like your creeping thing;
But your wise bees had stung him first to death.

THIRD MEMBER.

Hush, hush!
You wrong the Chancellor: the clauses added
To that same treaty which the Emperor sent us
Were mainly Gardiner's: that no foreigner
Hold office in the household, fleet, forts, army;
That if the Queen should die without a child,
The bond between the kingdoms be dissolved;
That Philip should not mix us any way
With his French wars —

SECOND MEMBER.

                    Ay, ay, but what security,
Good sir, for this, if Philip —

THIRD MEMBER.

                    Peace — the Queen,
Philip, and Pole.   [*All rise, and stand.*

Enter MARY, PHILIP, *and* POLE.

[GARDINER *conducts them to the three chairs*
    of state.   PHILIP *sits on the* QUEEN'S *left,*
    POLE *on her right.*

GARDINER.

Our short-lived sun, before his winter plunge,
Laughs at the last red leaf, and Andrew's Day.

MARY.

Should not this day be held in after years
More solemn than of old?

PHILIP.

                    Madam, my wish
Echoes your Majesty's.

POLE.

                    It shall be so.

GARDINER.

Mine echoes both your Graces'; (*aside*) but the
        Pope —
Can we not have the Catholic Church as well

Without as with the Italian? if we cannot,
Why, then the Pope.

            My lords of the upper house,
And ye, my masters, of the lower house,
Do ye stand fast by that which ye resolved?

VOICES.

We do.

GARDINER.

And be you all one mind to supplicate
The Legate here for pardon, and acknowledge
The primacy of the Pope?

VOICES.

            We are all one mind.

GARDINER.

Then must I play the vassal to this Pole.

                        [*Aside.*

    [*He draws a paper from under his robes and
        presents it to the* KING *and* QUEEN, *who
        look through it and return it to him ; then
        ascends a tribune, and reads.*

We, the Lords Spiritual and Temporal,
And Commons here in Parliament assembled,
Presenting the whole body of this realm

Of England, and dominions of the same,
Do make most humble suit unto your Majesties,
In our own name and that of all the state,
That by your gracious means and intercession
Our supplication be exhibited
To the Lord Cardinal Pole, sent here as Legate
From our most Holy Father Julius, Pope,
And from the Apostolic see of Rome;
And do declare our penitence and grief
For our long schism and disobedience,
Either in making laws and ordinances
Against the Holy Father's primacy,
Or else by doing or by speaking aught
Which might impugn or prejudice the same;
By this our supplication promising,
As well for our own selves as all the realm,
That now we be and ever shall be quick,
Under and with your Majesties' authorities,
To do to the utmost all that in us lies
Towards the abrogation and repeal
Of all such laws and ordinances made;
Whereon we humbly pray your Majesties,
As persons undefiled with our offence,
So to set forth this humble suit of ours

That we the rather by your intercession
May from the Apostolic see obtain,
Thro' this most reverend Father, absolution,
And full release from danger of all censures
Of Holy Church that we be fallen into,
So that we may, as children penitent,
Be once again received into the bosom
And unity of Universal Church;
And that this noble realm thro' after years
May in this unity and obedience
Unto the holy see and reigning Pope
Serve God and both your Majesties.

VOICES.

Amen.   [*All sit.*

[*He again presents the petition to the* KING
and QUEEN, *who hand it reverentially to*
POLE.

POLE (*sitting*).

This is the loveliest day that ever smiled
On England. All her breath should, incense-like,
Rise to the heavens in grateful praise of Him
Who now recalls her to His ancient fold.
Lo! once again God to this realm hath given

A token of His more especial Grace;
For as this people were the first of all
The islands call'd into the dawning church
Out of the dead, deep night of heathendom,
So now are these the first whom God hath given
Grace to repent and sorrow for their schism;
And if your penitence be not mockery,
Oh, how the blessed angels who rejoice
Over one saved do triumph at this hour
In the re-born salvation of a land
So noble!   [*A pause.*
              For ourselves we do protest
That our commission is to heal, not harm;
We come not to condemn, but reconcile;
We come not to compel, but call again;
We come not to destroy, but edify;
Nor yet to question things already done;
These are forgiven — matters of the past —
And range with jetsam and with offal thrown
Into the blind sea of forgetfulness.   [*A pause.*
Ye have reversed the attainder laid on us
By him who sack'd the house of God; and we,
Amplier than any field on our poor earth
Can render thanks in fruit for being sown,

Do here and now repay you sixty-fold,
A hundred, yea, a thousand thousand-fold,
With heaven for earth.

> [*Rising and stretching forth his hands. All
> kneel but* SIR RALPH BAGENHALL, *who
> rises and remains standing.*

                     The Lord who hath redeem'd us
With His own blood, and wash'd us from our
          sins,
To purchase for Himself a stainless bride;
He, whom the Father hath appointed Head
Of all His church, He by His mercy absolve
          you!   [*A pause.*
And we by that authority Apostolic
Given unto us, his Legate, by the Pope,
Our Lord and Holy Father, Julius,
God's Vicar and Vicegerent upon earth,
Do here absolve you and deliver you
And every one of you, and all the realm
And its dominions from all heresy,
All schism, and from all and every censure,
Judgment, and pain accruing thereupon;
And also we restore you to the bosom

And unity of Universal Church.

                   [*Turning to* GARDINER.

Our letters of commission will declare this
    plainlier.

       [QUEEN *heard sobbing. Cries of* AMEN!
       AMEN! *Some of the* MEMBERS *embrace*
       one another. All but SIR RALPH BAG-
       ENHALL *pass out into the neighbouring*
       chapel, whence is heard the Te Deum.

BAGENHALL.

We strove against the papacy from the first,
In William's time, in our first Edward's time,
And in my master Henry's time; but now,
The unity of Universal Church,
Mary would have it; and this Gardiner follows;
The unity of Universal Hell,
Philip would have it; and this Gardiner follows!
A Parliament of imitative apes!
Sheep at the gap which Gardiner takes, who not
Believes the Pope, nor any of them believe —
These spaniel-Spaniard English of the time
Who rub their fawning noses in the dust,
For that is Philip's gold-dust, and adore

This Vicar of their Vicar.   Would I had been
Born Spaniard!   I had held my head up then.
I am ashamed that I am Bagenhall,
English.

Enter OFFICER.

OFFICER.

Sir Ralph Bagenhall!

BAGENHALL.

What of that?

OFFICER.

You were the one sole man in either house
Who stood upright when both the houses fell.

BAGENHALL.

The houses fell!

OFFICER.

I mean the houses knelt

Before the Legate.

BAGENHALL.

Do not scrimp your phrase

But stretch it wider; say when England fell.

OFFICER.

I say you were the one sole man who stood.

BAGENHALL.

I am the one sole man in either house,
Perchance in England, loves her like a son.

OFFICER.

Well, you one man, because you stood upright,
Her Grace the Queen commands you to the
    Tower.

BAGENHALL.

As traitor, or as heretic, or for what?

OFFICER.

If any man in any way would be
The one man, he shall be so to his cost.

BAGENHALL.

What! will she have my head?

OFFICER.

                    A round fine likelier.
Your pardon.   [*Calling to Attendant.*
        By the river to the Tower.
                        [*Exeunt.*

SCENE IV. — WHITEHALL.   A ROOM IN THE
PALACE.

MARY, GARDINER, POLE, PAGET, BONNER, *etc.*

MARY.

The King and I, my Lords, now that all traitors
Against our royal state have lost the heads
Wherewith they plotted in their treasonous
   malice,
Have talk'd together, and are well agreed
That those old statutes touching Lollardism
To bring the heretic to the stake, should be
No longer a dead letter, but re-quicken'd.

ONE OF THE COUNCIL.

Why, what hath fluster'd Gardiner? how he rubs
His forelock!

PAGET.

    I have changed a word with him
In coming, and may change a word again.

GARDINER.

Madam, your Highness is our sun, the King
And you together our two suns in one;

And so the beams of both may shine upon us,
The faith that seem'd to droop will feel your
        light,
Lift head, and flourish; yet not light alone,
There must be heat—there must be heat enough
To scorch and wither heresy to the root.
For what saith Christ?   'Compel them to come
        in.'
And what saith Paul? 'I would they were cut off
That trouble you.'   Let the dead letter live!
Trace it in fire, that all the louts to whom
Their A B C is darkness, clowns and grooms
May read it! so you quash rebellion too,
For heretic and traitor are all one:
Two vipers of one breed — an amphisbæna,
Each end a sting.   Let the dead letter burn!

PAGET.

Yet there be some disloyal Catholics,
And many heretics loyal; heretic throats
Cried no God-bless-her to the Lady Jane,
But shouted in Queen Mary. So there be
Some traitor-heretic, there is axe and cord.
To take the lives of others that are loyal,

And by the churchman's pitiless doom of fire,
Were but a thankless policy in the crown,
Ay, and against itself; for there are many.

MARY.

If we could burn out heresy, my Lord Paget,
We reck not tho' we lost this crown of England —
Ay! tho' it were ten Englands!

GARDINER.

                        Right, your Grace.
Paget, you are all for this poor life of ours,
And care but little for the life to be.

PAGET.

I have some time, for curiousness, my Lord,
Watch'd children playing at *their* life to be,
And cruel at it, killing helpless flies;
Such is our time — all times for aught I know.

GARDINER.

We kill the heretics that sting the soul —
They, with right reason, flies that prick the flesh.

PAGET.

They had not reach'd right reason, little chil-
    dren!

They kill'd but for their pleasure and the power
They felt in killing.

GARDINER.

A spice of Satan, ha!
Why, good! what then? granted! — we are
    fallen creatures;
Look to your Bible, Paget! we are fallen.

PAGET.

I am but of the laity, my Lord Bishop,
And may not read your Bible, yet I found
One day a wholesome scripture, 'Little children,
Love one another.'

GARDINER.

Did you find a scripture,
'I come not to bring peace but a sword'? The
    sword
Is in her Grace's hand to smite with. Paget,
You stand up here to fight for heresy,
You are more than guess'd at as a heretic,
And on the steep-up track of the true faith
Your lapses are far seen.

PAGET.
                The faultless Gardiner!

MARY.

You brawl beyond the question; speak, Lord
    Legate!

POLE.

Indeed, I cannot follow with your Grace:
Rather would say — the shepherd doth not kill
The sheep that wander from his flock, but sends
His careful dog to bring them to the fold.
Look to the Netherlands, wherein have been
Such holocausts of heresy! to what end?
For yet the faith is not established there.

GARDINER.

The end's not come.

POLE.

                No — nor this way will come,
Seeing there lie two ways to every end,
A better and a worse — the worse is here
To persecute, because to persecute
Makes a faith hated, and is furthermore
No perfect witness of a perfect faith

In him who persecutes: when men are tost
On tides of strange opinion, and not sure
Of their own selves, they are wroth with their
    own selves,
And thence with others; then, who lights the
    faggot?
Not the full faith, no, but the lurking doubt.
Old Rome, that first made martyrs in the Church,
Trembled for her own gods, for these were
    trembling —
But when did our Rome tremble?

PAGET.

                Did she not
In Henry's time and Edward's?

POLE.

               What, my Lord!
The Church on Peter's rock? never! I have seen
A pine in Italy that cast its shadow
Athwart a cataract; firm stood the pine —
The cataract shook the shadow.   To my mind,
The cataract typed the headlong plunge and fall
Of heresy to the pit; the pine was Rome.

You see, my Lords,
It was the shadow of the Church that trembled;
Your church was but the shadow of a church,
Wanting the Papal mitre.

GARDINER (*muttering*).
Here be tropes.

POLE.

And tropes are good to clothe a naked truth,
And make it look more seemly.

GARDINER.
Tropes again!

POLE.

You are hard to please.   Then without tropes,
        my Lord,
An overmuch severeness, I repeat,
When faith is wavering makes the waverer pass
Into more settled hatred of the doctrines
Of those who rule, which hatred by and by
Involves the ruler (thus there springs to light
That Centaur of a monstrous Commonweal,
The traitor-heretic); then tho' some may quail,
Yet others are that dare the stake and fire,

And their strong torment bravely borne begets
An admiration and an indignation,
And hot desire to imitate; so the plague
Of schism spreads; were there but three or four
Of these misleaders, yet I would not say
Burn! and we cannot burn whole towns; they
      are many,
As my Lord Paget says.

GARDINER.
     Yet, my Lord Cardinal —

POLE.
I am your Legate; please you let me finish.
Methinks that under our Queen's regimen
We might go softlier than with crimson rowel
And streaming lash.   When Herod-Henry first
Began to batter at your English Church,
This was the cause, and hence the judgment on
      her.
She seethed with such adulteries, and the lives
Of many among your churchmen were so foul
That heaven wept and earth blush'd.   I would
      advise

That we should thoroughly cleanse the Church
    within
Before these bitter statutes be re-quicken'd.
So after that when she once more is seen
White as the light, the spotless bride of Christ,
Like Christ himself on Tabor, possibly
The Lutheran may be won to her again;
Till when, my Lords, I counsel tolerance.

GARDINER.

What, if a mad dog bit your hand, my Lord,
Would you not chop the bitten finger off,
Lest your whole body should madden with the
    poison?
I would not, were I Queen, tolerate the heretic,
No, not an hour.   The ruler of a land
Is bounden by his power and place to see
His people be not poison'd.   Tolerate them!
Why? do they tolerate you?   Nay, many of
    them
Would burn — have burnt each other; call they
    not
The one true faith a loathsome idol-worship?
Beware, Lord Legate, of a heavier crime

Than heresy is itself; beware, I say,
Lest men accuse you of indifference
To all faiths, all religion; for you know
Right well that you yourself have been supposed
Tainted with Lutheranism in Italy.

POLE (*angered*).

But you, my Lord, beyond all supposition,
In clear and open day were congruent
With that vile Cranmer in the accursed lie
Of good Queen Catharine's divorce — the spring
Of all those evils that have flow'd upon us;
For you yourself have truckled to the tyrant,
And done your best to bastardise our Queen,
For which God's righteous judgment fell upon
        you
In your five years of imprisonment, my Lord,
Under young Edward.   Who so bolster'd up
The gross King's headship of the Church, or
        more
Denied the Holy Father?

GARDINER.

                    Ha! what! eh?
But you, my Lord, a polish'd gentleman,

A bookman, flying from the heat and tussle,
You lived among your vines and oranges,
In your soft Italy yonder!   You were sent for,
You were appeal'd to, but you still preferr'd
Your learned leisure.   As for what I did,
I suffer'd and repented.   You, Lord Legate
And Cardinal-Deacon, have not now to learn
That even Saint Peter in his time of fear
Denied his Master, ay, and thrice, my Lord.

POLE.

But not for five-and-twenty years, my Lord.

GARDINER.

Ha! good! it seems then I was summon'd
     hither
But to be mock'd and baited.   Speak, friend
     Bonner,
And tell this learned Legate he lacks zeal.
The Church's evil is not as the King's,
Cannot be heal'd by stroking.   The mad bite
Must have the cautery — tell him — and at once.
What wouldst thou do hadst thou his power,
     thou

That layest so long in heretic bonds with me;
Wouldst thou not burn and blast them root and
        branch?

BONNER.

Ay, after you, my Lord.

GARDINER.

Nay, God's passion, before me! speak!

BONNER.

I am on fire until I see them flame.

GARDINER.

Ay, the psalm-singing weavers, cobblers, scum —
But this most noble prince Plantagenet,
Our good Queen's cousin — dallying over-seas
Even when his brother's, nay, his noble mother's,
Head fell —

POLE.

Peace, madman!
Thou stirrest up a grief thou canst not fathom.
Thou Christian Bishop, thou Lord Chancellor
Of England! no more rein upon thine anger

Than any child! Thou mak'st me much
    ashamed
That I was for a moment wroth at thee.

MARY.

I come for counsel and ye give me feuds,
Like dogs that, set to watch their master's gate,
Fall, when the thief is even within the walls,
To worrying one another.   My Lord Chancellor,
You have an old trick of offending us;
And but that you are art and part with us
In purging heresy, well we might, for this
Your violence and much roughness to the
    Legate,
Have shut you from our counsels.   Cousin Pole,
You are fresh from brighter lands.   Retire
    with me.
His Highness and myself (so you allow us)
Will let you learn in peace and privacy
What power this cooler sun of England hath
In breeding godless vermin.   And pray Heaven
That you may see according to our sight.
Come, cousin.

        [*Exeunt* QUEEN *and* POLE, *etc.*

GARDINER.

Pole has the Plantagenet face,
But not the force made them our mightiest kings.
Fine eyes — but melancholy, irresolute —
A fine beard, Bonner, a very full fine beard.
But a weak mouth, an indeterminate — ha?

BONNER.

Well, a weak mouth, perchance.

GARDINER.

And not like **thine**
To gorge a heretic whole, roasted or raw.

BONNER.

I'd do my best, my Lord; but yet the Legate
Is here as Pope and Master of the Church,
And if he go not with you —

GARDINER.

Tut, Master Bishop,
Our bashful Legate, saw'st not how he flush'd?
Touch him upon his old heretical talk,
He'll burn a diocese to prove his orthodoxy.
And let him call me truckler. In those times,

Thou knowest we had to dodge, or duck, or die;
I kept my head for use of Holy Church;
And see you, we shall have to dodge again,
And let the Pope trample our rights, and plunge
His foreign fist into our island Church
To plump the leaner pouch of Italy.
For a time, for a time.
Why? that these statutes may be put in force,
And that his fan may thoroughly purge his floor.

BONNER.

So then you hold the Pope —

GARDINER.

                               I hold the Pope!
What do I hold him? what do I hold the Pope?
Come, come, the morsel stuck — this Cardinal's
          fault —
I have gulpt it down. I am wholly for the Pope,
Utterly and altogether for the Pope,
The Eternal Peter of the changeless chair,
Crown'd slave of slaves, and mitred king of kings,
God upon earth! what more? what would you
          have?
Hence, let 's be gone.

Enter USHER.

USHER.

 Well that you be not gone,
My Lord.   The Queen, most wroth at first with
  you,
Is now content to grant you full forgiveness,
So that you crave full pardon of the Legate.
I am sent to fetch you.

GARDINER.

   Doth Pole yield, sir, ha?
Did you hear 'em? were you by?

USHER.

    I cannot tell you,
His bearing is so courtly-delicate;
And yet methinks he falters: their two Graces
Do so dear-cousin and royal-cousin him,
So press on him the duty which as Legate
He owes himself, and with such royal smiles —

GARDINER.

Smiles that burn men.   Bonner, it will be carried.
He falters, ha? 'fore God, we change and change;

Men now are bow'd and old, the doctors tell you,
At three-score years; then if we change at all
We needs must do it quickly; it is an age
Of brief life, and brief purpose, and brief patience,
As I have shown to-day.   I am sorry for it
If Pole be like to turn.   Our old friend Cranmer,
Your more especial love, hath turn'd so often,
He knows not where he stands, which, if this
        pass,
We two shall have to teach him ; let 'em look
        to it,
Cranmer and Hooper, Ridley and Latimer,
Rogers and Ferrar, for their time is come,
Their hour is hard at hand, their ' dies Iræ,'
Their ' dies Illa,' which will test their sect.
I feel it but a duty — you will find in it
Pleasure as well as duty, worthy Bonner, —
To test their sect.   Sir, I attend the Queen
To crave most humble pardon — of her most
Royal, Infallible, Papal Legate-cousin.

                                          [*Exeunt.*

SCENE V.—WOODSTOCK.

ELIZABETH, LADY IN WAITING.

ELIZABETH.

So they have sent poor Courtenay over-sea.

LADY.

And banish'd us to Woodstock, and the fields.
The colours of our Queen are green and white;
These fields are only green, they make me gape.

ELIZABETH.

There's white-thorn, girl.

LADY.

               Ay, for an hour in May.
But court is always May, buds out in masques,
Breaks into feather'd merriments, and flowers
In silken pageants. Why do they keep us here?
Why still suspect your Grace?

ELIZABETH.

               Hard upon both.
[*Writes on the window with a diamond.*

      Much suspected, of me
      Nothing proven can be.
           Quoth Elizabeth, prisoner.

LADY.

What hath your Highness written?

ELIZABETH.

A true rhyme.

LADY.

Cut with a diamond; so to last like truth.

ELIZABETH.

Ay, if truth last.

LADY.

But truth, they say, will out;
So it must last.   It is not like a word,
That comes and goes in uttering.

ELIZABETH.

Truth, a word!
The very Truth and very Word are one.
But truth of story, which I glanced at, girl,
Is like a word that comes from olden days,
And passes thro' the peoples: every tongue
Alters it passing, till it spells and speaks
Quite other than at first.

LADY.

    I do not follow.

ELIZABETH.

How many names, in the long sweep of time
That so foreshortens greatness, may but hang
On the chance mention of some fool that once
Brake bread with us, perhaps: and my poor
   chronicle
Is but of glass. Sir Henry Bedingfield
May split it for a spite.

LADY.

     God grant it last,
And witness to your Grace's innocence,
Till doomsday melt it!

ELIZABETH.

     Or a second fire,
Like that which lately crackled underfoot
And in this very chamber, fuse the glass,
And char us back again into the dust
We spring from. Never peacock against rain
Scream'd as you did for water.

LADY.

<blockquote>

And I got it.

I woke Sir Henry — and he's true to you —
I read his honest horror in his eyes.
</blockquote>

ELIZABETH.

<blockquote>
Or true to you?
</blockquote>

LADY.

<blockquote>

Sir Henry Bedingfield!

I will have no man true to me, your Grace,
But one that pares his nails; to me? the clown!
</blockquote>

ELIZABETH.

<blockquote>
Out, girl! you wrong a noble gentleman.
</blockquote>

LADY.

<blockquote>
For, like his cloak, his manners want the nap
And gloss of court; but of this fire he says,
Nay swears, it was no wicked wilfulness,
Only a natural chance.
</blockquote>

ELIZABETH.

<blockquote>

A chance — perchance

One of those wicked wilfuls that men make,
Nor shame to call it nature. Nay, I know
</blockquote>

They hunt my blood.   Save for my daily range
Among the pleasant fields of Holy Writ
I might despair.   But there hath some one
    come;
The house is all in movement.   Hence, and see.
                    [*Exit* Lady.

MILKMAID (*singing without*).

Shame upon you, Robin,
    Shame upon you now !
Kiss me would you ? with my hands
    Milking the cow ?
    Daisies grow again,
    Kingcups blow again,
And you came and kiss'd me milking the cow.

Robin came behind me,
    Kiss'd me well, I vow ;
Cuff him could I ? with my hands
    Milking the cow ?
    Swallows fly again,
    Cuckoos cry again,
And you came and kiss'd me milking the cow.

Come, Robin, Robin,
    Come and kiss me now ;
Help it can I ? with my hands
    Milking the cow ?
    Ringdoves coo again,
    All things woo again.
Come behind and kiss me milking the cow !

Elizabeth.

Right honest and red-cheek'd; Robin was violent,
And she was crafty — a sweet violence,
And a sweet craft.   I would I were a milkmaid,
To sing, love, marry, churn, brew, bake, and die,
Then have my simple headstone by the church,
And all things lived and ended honestly.
I could not if I would.   I am Harry's daughter:
Gardiner would have my head.   They are not
    sweet,
The violence and the craft that do divide
The world of nature; what is weak must lie;
The lion needs but roar to guard his young;
The lapwing lies, says 'here' when they are
    there.
Threaten the child, 'I'll scourge you if you
    did it:'
What weapon hath the child, save his soft tongue,
To say 'I did not'? and my rod's the block.
I never lay my head upon the pillow
But that I think, 'Wilt thou lie there to-morrow?'
How oft the falling axe, that never fell,
Hath shock'd me back into the daylight truth

That it may fall to-day! Those damp, black,
      dead
Nights in the Tower; dead — with the fear of
      death
Too dead even for a death-watch! Toll of a bell,
Stroke of a clock, the scurrying of a rat
Affrighted me, and then delighted me,
For there was life— And there was life in death—
The little murder'd princes, in a pale light,
Rose hand in hand, and whisper'd, 'Come away!
The civil wars are gone for evermore:
Thou last of all the Tudors, come away!
With us is peace!' The last? It was a dream;
I must not dream, not wink, but watch. She
      has gone,
Maid Marian to her Robin — by and by
Both happy! a fox may filch a hen by night,
And make a morning outcry in the yard;
But there's no Renard here to 'catch her trip-
      ping.'
Catch me who can; yet, sometime I have wish'd
That I were caught, and kill'd away at once
Out of the flutter. The gray rogue, Gardiner,
Went on his knees, and pray'd me to confess

In Wyatt's business, and to cast myself
Upon the good Queen's mercy; ay, when, my
    Lord?
God save the Queen!   My jailor —

Enter Sir Henry Bedingfield.

BEDINGFIELD.

            One, whose bolts,
That jail you from free life, bar you from death.
There haunt some Papist ruffians hereabout
Would murder you.

ELIZABETH.

          I thank you heartily, sir,
But I am royal, tho' your prisoner,
And God hath blest or cursed me with a nose —
Your boots are from the horses.

BEDINGFIELD.

             Ay, my Lady.
When next there comes a missive from the
    Queen
It shall be all my study for one hour
To rose and lavender my horsiness,
Before I dare to glance upon your Grace.

ELIZABETH.

A missive from the Queen: last time she wrote,
I had like to have lost my life: it takes my
    breath:
O God, sir, do you look upon your boots,
Are you so small a man? Help me: what
    think you,
Is it life or death?

BEDINGFIELD.

        I thought not on my boots;
The devil take all boots were ever made
Since man went barefoot! See, I lay it here,
For I will come no nearer to your Grace;
        [Laying down the letter.
And, whether it brings you bitter news or sweet,
And God hath given your Grace a nose or not,
I'll help you, if I may.

ELIZABETH.

        Your pardon, then;
It is the heat and narrowness of the cage
That makes the captive testy; with free wing
The world were all one Araby. Leave me now,
Will you, companion to myself, sir?

BEDINGFIELD.

Will I?

With most exceeding willingness, I will;
You know I never come till I be call'd.

[Exit.

ELIZABETH.

It lies there folded: is there venom in it?
A snake — and if I touch it, it may sting.
Come, come, the worst!
Best wisdom is to know the worst at once.

[Reads.

'It is the King's wish that you should wed
Prince Philibert of Savoy. You are to come to
Court on the instant; and think of this in your
coming.

'MARY THE QUEEN.'

Think! I have many thoughts;
I think there may be bird-lime here for me;
I think they fain would have me from the realm;
I think the Queen may never bear a child;
I think that I may be some time the Queen,
Then, Queen indeed: no foreign prince or priest
Should fill my throne, myself upon the steps.
I think I will not marry any one,

Specially not this landless Philibert
Of Savoy; but, if Philip menace me,
I think that I will play with Philibert, —
As once the Holy Father did with mine,
Before my father married my good mother, —
For fear of Spain.

Enter LADY.

LADY.

O Lord! your Grace, your Grace,
I feel so happy: it seems that we shall fly
These bald, blank fields, and dance into the sun
That shines on princes.

ELIZABETH.

Yet, a moment since,
I wish'd myself the milkmaid singing here,
To kiss and cuff among the birds and flowers —
A right rough life and healthful.

LADY.

But the wench
Hath her own troubles; she is weeping now;
For the wrong Robin took her at her word.

Then the cow kick'd, and all her milk was spilt.
Your Highness such a milkmaid?

Elizabeth.

I had kept
My Robins and my cows in sweeter order
Had I been such.

Lady (*slyly*).

And had your Grace a Robin?

Elizabeth.

Come, come, you are chill here; you want the
　　sun
That shines at court; make ready for the journey.
Pray God, we 'scape the sunstroke.   Ready at
　　once.　　　　　　　　　　　　　　*[Exeunt.*

SCENE VI. — London.   A Room in the
Palace.

Lord Petre *and* Lord William Howard.

Petre.

You cannot see the Queen.   Renard denied her
Even now to me.

HOWARD.

Their Flemish go-between
And all-in-all.   I came to thank her Majesty
For freeing my friend Bagenhall from the Tower;
A grace to me !   Mercy, that herb-of-grace,
Flowers now but seldom.

PETRE.

Only now, perhaps,
Because the Queen hath been three days in tears
For Philip's going — like the wild hedge-rose
Of a soft winter, possible, not probable,
However you have proven it.

HOWARD.

I must see her.

Enter RENARD.

RENARD.

My Lords, you cannot see her Majesty.

HOWARD.

Why, then the King ! for I would have him bring
         it
Home to the leisure wisdom of his Queen,

Before he go, that since these statutes past,
Gardiner out-Gardiners Gardiner in his heat,
Bonner cannot out-Bonner his own self —
Beast! — but they play with fire as children do,
And burn the house. I know that these are breeding
      breeding
A fierce resolve and fixt heart-hate in men
Against the King, the Queen, the Holy Father,
The faith itself.   Can I not see him?

RENARD.
               Not now.
And in all this, my Lord, her Majesty
Is flint of flint; you may strike fire from her,
Not hope to melt her.   I will give your message.
            [*Exeunt* Petre *and* Howard.

Enter Philip (*musing*).

PHILIP.
She will not have Prince Philibert of Savoy,
I talk'd with her in vain — says she will live
And die true maid — a goodly creature too.
Would *she* had been the Queen! yet she must
      have him;

She troubles England: that she breathes in
    England
Is life and lungs to every rebel birth
That passes out of embryo.

               Simon Renard! —
This Howard, whom they fear, what was he
    saying?

           RENARD.

What your imperial father said, my liege,
To deal with heresy gentlier.   Gardiner burns,
And Bonner burns; and it would seem this
    people
Care more for our brief life in their wet land
Than yours in happier Spain.   I told my Lord
He should not vex her Highness; she would
    say
These are the means God works with, that His
    church
May flourish.

           PHILIP.

        Ay, sir, but in statesmanship
To strike too soon is oft to miss the blow.
Thou knowest I bade my chaplain, Castro, preach
Against these burnings.

RENARD.

And the Emperor
Approved you, and, when last he wrote, declared
His comfort in your Grace that you were bland
And affable to men of all estates,
In hope to charm them from their hate of Spain.

PHILIP.

In hope to crush all heresy under Spain.
But, Renard, I am sicker staying here
Than any sea could make me passing hence,
Tho' I be ever deadly sick at sea.
So sick am I with biding for this child.
Is it the fashion in this clime for women
To go twelve months in bearing of a child?
The nurses yawn'd, the cradle gaped, they led
Processions, chanted litanies, clash'd their bells,
Shot off their lying cannon, and her priests
Have preach'd, the fools, of this fair prince to
        come,
Till, by Saint James, I find myself the fool.
Why do you lift your eyebrow at me thus?

RENARD.

I never saw your Highness moved till now.

PHILIP.

So weary am I of this wet land of theirs,
And every soul of man that breathes therein.

RENARD.

My liege, we must not drop the mask before
The masquerade is over —

PHILIP.

                              Have I dropt it?
I have but shown a loathing face to you,
Who knew it from the first.

Enter MARY.

MARY (*aside*).

                    With Renard.   Still
Parleying with Renard, all the day with Renard,
And scarce a greeting all the day for me —
And goes to-morrow.   [*Exit* MARY.

PHILIP (*to* RENARD, *who advances to him*).
                    Well, sir, is there more?

RENARD (*who has perceived the* QUEEN).
May Simon Renard speak a single word?

PHILIP.

Ay.

RENARD.

And be forgiven for it?

PHILIP.

Simon Renard
Knows me too well to speak a single word
That could not be forgiven.

RENARD.

Well, my liege,
Your Grace hath a most chaste and loving wife.

PHILIP.

Why not? The Queen of Philip should be
chaste.

RENARD.

Ay, but, my Lord, you know what Virgil sings,
Woman is various and most mutable.

PHILIP.

She play the harlot! never.

RENARD.

No, sire, no,
Not dream'd of by the rabidest gospeller.

There was a paper thrown into the palace,
' The King hath wearied of his barren bride.'
She came upon it, read it, and then rent it,
With all the rage of one who hates a truth
He cannot but allow.   Sire, I would have you —
What should I say, I cannot pick my words —
Be somewhat less — majestic to your Queen.

PHILIP.

Am I to change my manners, Simon Renard,
Because these islanders are brutal beasts?
Or would you have me turn a sonneteer,
And warble those brief-sighted eyes of hers?

RENARD.

Brief-sighted tho' they be, I have seen them, sire,
When you perchance were trifling royally
With some fair dame of court, suddenly fill
With such fierce fire — had it been fire indeed
It would have burnt both speakers.

PHILIP.

                          Ay, and then?

RENARD.

Sire, might it not be policy in some matter
Of small importance now and then to cede
A point to her demand?

PHILIP.

Well, I am going.

RENARD.

For should her love when you are gone, my
      liege,
Witness these papers, there will not be wanting
Those that will urge her injury — should her
      love —
And I have known such women more than one —
Veer to the counterpoint, and jealousy
Hath in it an alchemic force to fuse
Almost into one metal love and hate, —
And she impress her wrongs upon her Council,
And these again upon her Parliament —
We are not loved here, and would be then
      perhaps
Not so well holpen in our wars with France,
As else we might be — here she comes.

Enter MARY.

MARY.

O Philip!

Nay, must you go indeed?

PHILIP.

Madam, I must.

MARY.

The parting of a husband and a wife
Is like the cleaving of a heart; one half
Will flutter here, one there.

PHILIP.

You say true, Madam.

MARY.

The Holy Virgin will not have me yet
Lose the sweet hope that I may bear a prince.
If such a prince were born and you not here!

PHILIP.

I should be here if such a prince were born.

MARY.

But must you go?

PHILIP.

Madam, you know my father,
Retiring into cloistral solitude
To yield the remnant of his years to heaven,
Will shift the yoke and weight of all the world
From off his neck to mine. We meet at Brussels.
But since mine absence will not be for long,
Your Majesty shall go to Dover with me,
And wait my coming back.

MARY.

To Dover? no,
I am too feeble. I will go to Greenwich,
So you will have me with you; and there watch
All that is gracious in the breath of heaven
Draw with your sails from our poor land, and
pass
And leave me, Philip, with my prayers for you.

PHILIP.

And doubtless I shall profit by your prayers.

MARY.

Methinks that would you tarry one day more
(The news was sudden) I could mould myself
To bear your going better; will you do it?

194 QUEEN MARY. [ACT III.

PHILIP.

Madam, a day may sink or save a realm.

MARY.

A day may save a heart from breaking too.

PHILIP.

Well, Simon Renard, shall we stop a day?

RENARD.

Your Grace's business will not suffer, sire,
For one day more, so far as I can tell.

PHILIP.

Then one day more to please her Majesty.

MARY.

The sunshine sweeps across my life again.
Oh, if I knew you felt this parting, Philip,
As I do!

PHILIP.

By Saint James I do protest,
Upon the faith and honour of a Spaniard,
I am vastly grieved to leave your Majesty.
Simon, is supper ready?

RENARD.

Ay, my liege,

I saw the covers laying.

PHILIP.

Let us have it.

[*Exeunt.*

ACT IV.

SCENE I. — A ROOM IN THE PALACE.

MARY, CARDINAL POLE.

MARY.

What have you there?

POLE.

    So please your Majesty,
A long petition from the foreign exiles
To spare the life of Cranmer. Bishop Thirlby,
And my Lord Paget and Lord William Howard,
Crave, in the same cause, hearing of your Grace.
Hath he not written himself — infatuated —
To sue you for his life?

MARY.

    His life? Oh, no;
Not sued for that — he knows it were in vain.
But so much of the anti-papal leaven
Works in him yet, he hath pray'd me not to
  sully

Mine own prerogative, and degrade the realm
By seeking justice at a stranger's hand
Against my natural subject.   King and Queen,
To whom he owes his loyalty after God,
Shall these accuse him to a foreign prince?
Death would not grieve him more.   I cannot be
True to this realm of England and the Pope
Together, says the heretic.

> POLE.
>> And there errs;
As he hath ever err'd thro' vanity.
A secular kingdom is but as the body
Lacking a soul; and in itself a beast.
The Holy Father in a secular kingdom
Is as the soul descending out of heaven
Into a body generate.

> MARY.
>> Write to him, then.

> POLE.
I will.

> MARY.
And sharply, Pole.

POLE.

Here come the Cranmerites!

Enter THIRLBY, LORD PAGET, LORD WILLIAM
HOWARD.

HOWARD.

Health to your Grace!   Good morrow, my
    Lord Cardinal;
We make our humble prayer unto your Grace
That Cranmer may withdraw to foreign parts,
Or into private life within the realm.
In several bills and declarations, **Madam,**
He hath recanted all his heresies.

PAGET.

Ay, ay; if Bonner have not forged the bills.

                                     [*Aside.*

MARY.

Did not More die, and Fisher? he must burn.

HOWARD.

He hath recanted, Madam.

MARY.

                        The better for him.
He burns in Purgatory, not in Hell.

HOWARD.

Ay, ay, your Grace; but it was never seen
That any one recanting thus at full,
As Cranmer hath, came to the fire on earth.

MARY.

It will be seen now, then.

THIRLBY.

O Madam, Madam!

I thus implore you, low upon my knees,
To reach the hand of mercy to my friend.
I have err'd with him; with him I have recanted.
What human reason is there why my friend
Should meet with lesser mercy than myself?

MARY.

My Lord of Ely, this.   After a riot
We hang the leaders, let their following go.
Cranmer is head and father of these heresies,
New learning as they call it; yea, may God
Forget me at most need when I forget
Her foul divorce — my sainted mother — No! —

HOWARD.

Ay, ay, but mighty doctors doubted there.
The Pope himself waver'd; and more than one

Row'd in that galley — Gardiner to wit,
Whom truly I deny not to have been
Your faithful friend and trusty councillor.
Hath not your Highness ever read his book,
His tractate upon True Obedience,
Writ by himself and Bonner?

MARY.

                I will take
Such order with all bad, heretical books
That none shall hold them in his house and
      live,
Henceforward. No, my Lord.

HOWARD.

                Then never read it.
The truth is here.   Your father was a man
Of such colossal kinghood, yet so courteous,
Except when wroth, you scarce could meet his
      eye
And hold your own; and were he wroth indeed,
You held it less, or not at all.   I say,
Your father had a will that beat men down;
Your father had a brain that beat men down —

POLE.

Not me, my Lord.

HOWARD.

        No, for you were not here;
You sit upon this fallen Cranmer's throne;
And it would more become you, my Lord
      Legate,
To join a voice, so potent with her Highness,
To ours in plea for Cranmer than to stand
On naked self-assertion.

MARY.

        All your voices
Are waves on flint.   The heretic must burn.

HOWARD.

Yet once he saved your Majesty's own life;
Stood out against the King in your behalf,
At his own peril.

MARY.

       I know not if he did;
And if he did I care not, my Lord Howard.
My life is not so happy, no such boon,

That I should spare to take a heretic priest's,
Who saved it or not saved. Why do you vex
    me?

PAGET.

Yet to save Cranmer were to serve the Church,
Your Majesty's I mean; he is effaced,
Self-blotted out; so wounded in his honour,
He can but creep down into some dark hole
Like a hurt beast, and hide himself and die;
But if you burn him, — well, your Highness
    knows
The saying, ' Martyr's blood — seed of the
    Church.'

MARY.

Of the true Church; but his is none, nor will be.
You are too politic for me, my Lord Paget.
And if he have to live so loath'd a life,
It were more merciful to burn him now.

THIRLBY.

Oh, yet relent!   Oh, Madam, if you knew him
As I do, ever gentle, and so gracious,
With all his learning —

MARY.

                    Yet a heretic still.
His learning makes his burning the more just.

THIRLBY.

So worshipt of all those that came across him ;
The stranger at his hearth, and all his house —

MARY.

His children and his concubine, belike.

THIRLBY.

To do him any wrong was to beget
A kindness from him, for his heart was rich,
Of such fine mould that if you sow'd therein
The seed of Hate, it blossom'd Charity.

POLE.

' After his kind it costs him nothing,' there 's
An old world English adage to the point.
These are but natural graces, my good Bishop,
Which in the Catholic garden are as flowers,
But on the heretic dunghill only weeds.

HOWARD.

Such weeds make dunghills gracious.

MARY.

Enough, my Lords.
It is God's will, the Holy Father's will,
And Philip's will, and mine, that he should
    burn.
He is pronounced anathema.

HOWARD.

Farewell, Madam,
God grant you ampler mercy at your call
Than you have shown to Cranmer.

[*Exeunt* LORDS.

POLE.

After this,
Your Grace will hardly care to overlook
This same petition of the foreign exiles
For Cranmer's life.

MARY.

Make out the writ to-night.
[*Exeunt.*

SCENE II. — OXFORD.   CRANMER IN PRISON.

CRANMER.

Last night, I dream'd the faggots were alight,
And that myself was fasten'd to the stake,
And found it all a visionary flame,
Cool as the light in old decaying wood;
And then King Harry look'd from out a cloud,
And bade me have good courage; and I heard
An angel cry, ' There is more joy in Heaven,' —
And after that, the trumpet of the dead.
                    [*Trumpets without.*
Why, there are trumpets blowing now : what is it?

Enter FATHER COLE.

COLE.

Cranmer, I come to question you again;
Have you remain'd in the true Catholic faith
I left you in?
                    CRANMER.
                In the true Catholic faith,
By Heaven's grace, I am more and more con-
    firm'd.
Why are the trumpets blowing, Father Cole?

COLE.

Cranmer, it is decided by the Council
That you to-day should read your recantation
Before the people in Saint Mary's Church.
And there be many heretics in the town,
Who loathe you for your late return to Rome,
And might assail you passing through the street,
And tear you piecemeal: so you have a guard.

CRANMER.

Or seek to rescue me.   I thank the Council.

COLE.

Do you lack any money?

CRANMER.

                Nay, why should I?
The prison fare is good enough for me.

COLE.

Ay, but to give the poor.

CRANMER.

              Hand it me, then!
I thank you.

COLE.

For a little space, farewell;
Until I see you in Saint Mary's Church.

[*Exit* COLE.

CRANMER.

It is against all precedent to burn
One who recants; they mean to pardon me.
To give the poor — they give the poor who die.
Well, burn me or not burn me I am fixt;
It is but a communion, not a mass:
A holy supper, not a sacrifice;
No man can make his Maker — Villa Garcia.

Enter VILLA GARCIA.

VILLA GARCIA.

Pray you write out this paper for me, Cranmer.

CRANMER.

Have I not writ enough to satisfy you?

VILLA GARCIA.

It is the last.

CRANMER.

Give it me, then.   [*He writes.*

VILLA GARCIA.

                              Now sign.

CRANMER.

I have sign'd enough, and I will sign no more.

VILLA GARCIA.

It is no more than what you have sign'd already,
The public form thereof.

CRANMER.

                    It may be so;
I sign it with my presence, if I read it.

VILLA GARCIA.

But this is idle of you.   Well, sir, well,
You are to beg the people to pray for you;
Exhort them to a pure and virtuous life;
Declare the Queen's right to the throne; confess
Your faith before all hearers; and retract
That Eucharistic doctrine in your book.
Will you not sign it now?

CRANMER.

                    No, Villa Garcia,
I sign no more.   Will they have mercy on me?

VILLA GARCIA.

Have you good hopes of mercy! So, farewell.
[*Exit.*

CRANMER.

Good hopes, not theirs, have I that I am fixt,
Fixt beyond fall; however, in strange hours,
After the long brain-dazing colloquies,
And thousand-times recurring argument
Of those two friars ever in my prison,
When left alone in my despondency,
Without a friend, a book, my faith would seem
Dead or half-drown'd, or else swam heavily
Against the huge corruptions of the Church,
Monsters of mistradition, old enough
To scare me into dreaming, ' What am I,
Cranmer, against whole ages?' was it so,
Or am I slandering my most inward friend,
To veil the fault of my most outward foe —
The soft and tremulous coward in the flesh?
O higher, holier, earlier, purer church,
I have found thee and not leave thee any more.
It is but a communion, not a mass —
No sacrifice, but a life-giving feast!

VOL. XI. — 14

(*Writes.*)   So, so ; this will I say — thus will I
    pray.   [*Puts up the paper.*

Enter BONNER.

BONNER.

Good day, old friend; what, you look somewhat
    worn ;
And yet it is a day to test your health
Even at the best: I scarce have spoken with you
Since when? — your degradation.   At your
    trial
Never stood up a bolder man than you ;
You would not cap the Pope's commissioner —
Your learning, and your stoutness, and your
    heresy,
Dumbfounded half of us.   So, after that,
We had to dis-archbishop and unlord,
And make you simple Cranmer once again.
The common barber clipt your hair, and I
Scraped from your finger-points the holy oil ;
And worse than all, you had to kneel to *me ;*
Which was not pleasant for you, Master Cran-
    mer.
Now you, that would not recognise the Pope,

And you, that would not own the Real Presence,
Have found a real presence in the stake,
Which frights you back into the ancient faith;
And so you have recanted to the Pope.
How are the mighty fallen, Master Cranmer!

CRANMER.

You have been more fierce against the Pope
    than I;
But why fling back the stone he strikes me with?
                        [*Aside.*
O Bonner, if I ever did you kindness —
Power hath been given you to try faith by fire —
Pray you, remembering how yourself have
    changed,
Be somewhat pitiful, after I have gone,
To the poor flock — to women and to children —
That when I was archbishop held with me.

BONNER.

Ay — gentle as they call you — live or die!
Pitiful to this pitiful heresy?
I must obey the Queen and Council, man.
Win thro' this day with honour to yourself,

And I 'll say something for you — so — good-
    bye.   [*Exit.*

CRANMER.

This hard coarse man of old hath crouch'd to
    me
Till I myself was half ashamed for him.

Enter THIRLBY.

Weep not, good Thirlby.

THIRLBY.

           Oh, my Lord, my Lord!
My heart is no such block as Bonner's is:
Who would not weep?

CRANMER.

           Why do you so my-lord me,
Who am disgraced?

THIRLBY.

           On earth; but saved in heaven
By your recanting.

CRANMER.

           Will they burn me, Thirlby?

THIRLBY.

Alas, they will; these burnings will not help
The purpose of the faith; but my poor voice
Against them is a whisper to the roar
Of a spring-tide.

CRANMER.

And they will surely burn me?

THIRLBY.

Ay; and besides will have you in the church
Repeat your recantation in the ears
Of all men, to the saving of their souls,
Before your execution.   May God help you
Thro' that hard hour!

CRANMER.

And may God bless you, Thirlby!
Well, they shall hear my recantation there.

[*Exit* THIRLBY.

Disgraced, dishonour'd! — not by them, indeed,
By mine own self — by mine own hand!
O thin-skinn'd hand and jutting veins, 'twas you
That sign'd the burning of poor Joan of Kent;
But then she was a witch.   You have written
        much,

But you were never raised to plead for Frith,
Whose dogmas I have reach'd : he was deliver'd
To the secular arm to burn; and there was
      Lambert;
Who can foresee himself? truly these burnings,
As Thirlby says, are profitless to the burners,
And help the other side.   You shall burn too,
Burn first when I am burnt.
Fire — inch by inch to die in agony! Latimer
Had a brief end — not Ridley.   Hooper burn'd
Three-quarters of an hour.   Will my faggots
Be wet as his were?   It is a day of rain.
I will not muse upon it.
My fancy takes the burner's part, and makes
The fire seem even crueller than it is.
No, I not doubt that God will give me strength,
Albeit I have denied him.

Enter SOTO *and* VILLA GARCIA.

VILLA GARCIA.

                  We are ready
To take you to Saint Mary's, Master Cranmer.

CRANMER.

And I : lead on ; ye loose me from my bonds.

                              [Exeunt.

SCENE III. — ST. MARY'S CHURCH.

COLE *in the Pulpit*, LORD WILLIAMS OF THAME *presiding.* LORD WILLIAM HOWARD, LORD PAGET, *and others.* CRANMER *enters between* SOTO *and* VILLA GARCIA, *and the whole Choir strike up*, ' Nunc Dimittis.' CRANMER *is set upon a Scaffold before the people.*

COLE.

Behold him —
  [A pause : people in the foreground.

PEOPLE.

Oh, unhappy sight!

FIRST PROTESTANT.

See how the tears run down his fatherly face.

SECOND PROTESTANT.

James, didst thou ever see a carrion crow
Stand watching a sick beast before he dies?

FIRST PROTESTANT.

Him perch'd up there? I wish some thunderbolt
Would make this Cole a cinder, pulpit and all.

COLE.

Behold him, brethren : he hath cause to weep ! —
So have we all: weep with him if ye will,
Yet —
It is expedient for one man to die,
Yea, for the people, lest the people die.
Yet wherefore should he die that hath return'd
To the one Catholic Universal Church,
Repentant of his errors?

PROTESTANT MURMURS.

Ay, tell us that.

COLE.

Those of the wrong side will despise the man,
Deeming him one that thro' the fear of death
Gave up his cause, except he seal his faith
In sight of all with flaming martyrdom.

CRANMER.

Ay.

COLE.

Ye hear him, and albeit there may seem
According to the canons pardon due
To him that so repents, yet are there causes
Wherefore our Queen and Council at this time

Adjudge him to the death. He hath been a
    traitor,
A shaker and confounder of the realm;
And when the King's divorce was sued at Rome,
He here, this heretic metropolitan,
As if he had been the Holy Father, sat
And judged it.   Did I call him heretic?
A huge heresiarch! never was it known
That any man so writing, preaching so,
So poisoning the Church, so long continuing,
Hath found his pardon; therefore he must die,
For warning and example.
                  Other reasons
There be for this man's ending, which our Queen
And Council at this present deem it not
Expedient to be known.

           Protestant Murmurs.
                  I warrant you.

           Cole.
Take therefore, all, example by this man,
For if our Holy Queen not pardon him,
Much less shall others in like cause escape,
That all of you, the highest as the lowest,

May learn there is no power against the Lord.
There stands a man, once of so high degree,
Chief prelate of our Church, archbishop, first
In Council, second person in the realm,
Friend for so long time of a mighty King;
And now ye see downfallen and debased
From councillor to caitiff — fallen so low,
The leprous flutterings of the byway, scum
And offal of the city, would not change
Estates with him; in brief, so miserable,
There is no hope of better left for him,
No place for worse.

             Yet, Cranmer, be thou glad.
This is the work of God.   He is glorified
In thy conversion: lo! thou art reclaim'd;
He brings thee home: nor fear but that to-day
Thou shalt receive the penitent thief's award,
And be with Christ the Lord in Paradise.
Remember how God made the fierce fire seem
To those three children like a pleasant dew.
Remember, too,
The triumph of Saint Andrew on his cross,
The patience of Saint Lawrence in the fire.
Thus, if thou call on God and all the saints,

God will beat down the fury of the flame,
Or give thee saintly strength to undergo.
And for thy soul shall masses here be sung
By every priest in Oxford.   Pray for him.

CRANMER.

Ay, one and all, dear brothers, pray for me ;
Pray with one breath, one heart, one soul for me.

COLE.

And now, lest any one among you doubt
The man's conversion and remorse of heart,
Yourselves shall hear him speak.   Speak, Master
        Cranmer,
Fulfil your promise made me, and proclaim
Your true undoubted faith, that all may hear.

CRANMER.

And that I will.   O God, Father of Heaven !
O Son of God, Redeemer of the world !
O Holy Ghost, proceeding from them both !
Three persons and one God, have mercy on me,
Most miserable sinner, wretched man !
I have offended against heaven and earth
More grievously than any tongue can tell.

Then whither should I flee for any help?
I am ashamed to lift my eyes to heaven,
And I can find no refuge upon earth.
Shall I despair then? — God forbid! O God,
For Thou art merciful, refusing none
That come to Thee for succour, unto Thee,
Therefore, I come; humble myself to Thee;
Saying, O Lord God, although my sins be great,
For Thy great mercy have mercy! O God the
          Son,
Not for slight faults alone, when Thou becamest
Man in the Flesh, was the great mystery
          wrought;
O God the Father, not for little sins
Didst Thou yield up Thy Son to human death;
But for the greatest sin that can be sinn'd,
Yea, even such as mine, incalculable,
Unpardonable, — sin against the light,
The truth of God, which I had proven and known.
Thy mercy must be greater than all sin.
Forgive me, Father, for no merit of mine,
But that Thy name by man be glorified,
And Thy most blessed Son's, who died for man.
     Good people, every man at time of death

Would fain set forth some saying that may live
After his death and better humankind;
For death gives life's last word a power to live,
And, like the stone-cut epitaph, remain
After the vanish'd voice, and speak to men.
God grant me grace to glorify my God!
And first I say it is a grievous case,
Many so dote upon this bubble world,
Whose colours in a moment break and fly,
They care for nothing else.   What saith Saint
        John?
' Love of this world is hatred against God.'
Again, I pray you all that, next to God,
You do unmurmuringly and willingly
Obey your King and Queen, and not for dread
Of these alone, but from the fear of Him
Whose ministers they be to govern you.
Thirdly, I pray you all to live together
Like brethren; yet what hatred Christian men
Bear to each other, seeming not as brethren,
But mortal foes!   But do you good to all
As much as in you lieth.   Hurt no man more
Than you would harm your loving natural
        brother

Of the same roof, same breast.   If any do,
Albeit he think himself at home with God,
Of this be sure, he is whole worlds away.

PROTESTANT MURMURS.

What sort of brothers then be those that lust
To burn each other?

WILLIAMS.

Peace among you, there!

CRANMER.

Fourthly, to those that own exceeding wealth,
Remember that sore saying spoken once
By Him that was the truth, ' How hard it is
For the rich man to enter into heaven; '
Let all rich men remember that hard word.
I have not time for more: if ever, now
Let them flow forth in charity, seeing now
The poor so many, and all food so dear.
Long have I lain in prison, yet have heard
Of all their wretchedness.   Give to the poor,
Ye give to God.   He is with us in the poor.
    And now, and forasmuch as I have come
To the last end of life, and thereupon

Hangs all my past, and all my life to be,
Either to live with Christ in heaven with joy,
Or to be still in pain with devils in hell;
And, seeing in a moment, I shall find

          [Pointing upwards.

Heaven or else hell ready to swallow me,

          [Pointing downwards.

I shall declare to you my very faith
Without all colour.

COLE.

Hear him, my good brethren.

CRANMER.

I do believe in God, Father of all;
In every article of the Catholic faith,
And every syllable taught us by our Lord,
His prophets, and apostles, in the Testaments,
Both Old and New.

COLE.

Be plainer, Master Cranmer.

CRANMER.

And now I come to the great cause that weighs
Upon my conscience more than anything

Or said or done in all my life by me;
For there be writings I have set abroad
Against the truth I knew within my heart,
Written for fear of death, to save my life,
If that might be; the papers by my hand
Sign'd since my degradation — by this hand

               [*Holding out his right hand.*

Written and sign'd — I here renounce them all;
And, since my hand offended, having written
Against my heart, my hand shall first be burnt,
So I may come to the fire.   [*Dead silence.*

PROTESTANT MURMURS.

FIRST PROTESTANT.

I knew it would be so.

SECOND PROTESTANT.

            Our prayers are heard!

THIRD PROTESTANT.

God bless him!

CATHOLIC MURMURS.

         Out upon him! out upon him!
Liar! dissembler! traitor! to the fire!

WILLIAMS (*raising his voice*).

You know that you recanted all you said
Touching the sacrament in that same book
You wrote against my Lord of Winchester;
Dissemble not; play the plain Christian man.

CRANMER.

Alas, my Lord,
I have been a man loved plainness all my life;
I *did* dissemble, but the hour has come
For utter truth and plainness; wherefore, I say,
I hold by all I wrote within that book.
Moreover,
As for the Pope, I count him Antichrist,
With all his devil's doctrines, and refuse,
Reject him, and abhor him.   I have said.

    [*Cries on all sides*, ' Pull him down! Away
      with him!'

COLE.

Ay, stop the heretic's mouth!   Hale him away!

WILLIAMS.

Harm him not, harm him not! have him to the
    fire!

[CRANMER *goes out between Two Friars, smil-*
ing; hands are reached to him from the
crowd. LORD WILLIAM HOWARD *and* LORD
PAGET *are left alone in the church.*

PAGET.

The nave and aisles all empty as a fool's jest!
No, here's Lord William Howard.   What, my
          Lord,
You have not gone to see the burning?

HOWARD.

                              Fie!
To stand at ease, and stare as at a show,
And watch a good man burn.   Never again.
I saw the deaths of Latimer and Ridley.
Moreover, tho' a Catholic, I would not,
For the pure honour of our common nature,
Hear what I might — another recantation
Of Cranmer at the stake.

PAGET.

                    You'd not hear that.
He pass'd out smiling, and he walk'd upright;
His eye was like a soldier's, whom the general
He looks to and he leans on as his God,

Hath rated for some backwardness and bidden
        him
Charge one against a thousand, and the man
Hurls his soil'd life against the pikes and dies.

HOWARD.

Yet that he might not after all those papers
Of recantation yield again, who knows?

PAGET.

Papers of recantation!   Think you then
That Cranmer read all papers that he sign'd?
Or sign'd all those they tell us that he sign'd?
Nay, I trow not: and you shall see, my Lord,
That howsoever hero-like the man
Dies in the fire, this Bonner or another
Will in some lying fashion misreport
His ending to the glory of their church.
And you saw Latimer and Ridley die?
Latimer was eighty, was he not? his best
Of life was over then.

HOWARD.

                His eighty years
Look'd somewhat crooked on him in his frieze;

But after they had stript him to his shroud,
He stood upright, a lad of twenty-one,
And gather'd with his hands the starting flame,
And wash'd his hands and all his face therein,
Until the powder suddenly blew him dead.
Ridley was longer burning; but he died
As manfully and boldly, and, 'fore God,
I know them heretics, but right English ones.
If ever, as heaven grant, we clash with Spain,
Our Ridley-soldiers and our Latimer-sailors
Will teach her something.

PAGET.

                    Your mild Legate Pole
Will tell you that the devil helpt them thro' it.
          [*A murmur of the Crowd in the distance.*
Hark, how those Roman wolf-dogs howl and bay
          him!
HOWARD.

Might it not be the other side rejoicing
In his brave end?

PAGET.

          They are too crush'd, too broken,
They can but weep in silence.

HOWARD.

                Ay, ay, Paget,
They have brought it in large measure on them-
    selves.
Have I not heard them mock the blessed Host
In songs so lewd the beast might roar his claim
To being in God's image, more than they?
Have I not seen the gamekeeper, the groom,
Gardener, and huntsman, in the parson's place,
The parson from his own spire swung out dead,
And Ignorance crying in the streets, and all
    men
Regarding her?　I say they have drawn the fire
On their own heads: yet, Paget, I do hold
The Catholic, if he have the greater right,
Hath been the crueller.

PAGET.

               Action and reaction,
The miserable see-saw of our child-world,
Make us despise it at odd hours, my Lord.
Heaven help that this reaction not react
Yet fiercelier under Queen Elizabeth,
So that she come to rule us.

HOWARD.

The world's mad.

PAGET.

My Lord, the world is like a drunken man,
Who cannot move straight to his end, but
    reels
Now to the right, then as far to the left,
Push'd by the crowd beside — and underfoot
An earthquake; for since Henry for a doubt —
Which a young lust had clapt upon the back,
Crying, 'Forward!' — set our old church rock-
    ing, men
Have hardly known what to believe, or whether
They should believe in anything; the currents
So shift and change, they see not how they are
    borne,
Nor whither.   I conclude the King a beast;
Verily a lion if you will — the world
A most obedient beast and fool — myself
Half beast and fool as appertaining to it;
Altho' your Lordship hath as little of each
Cleaving to your original Adam-clay
As may be consonant with mortality.

HOWARD.

We talk and Cranmer suffers.
The kindliest man I ever knew; see, see,
I speak of him in the past.   Unhappy land!
Hard-natured Queen, half-Spanish in herself,
And grafted on the hard-grain'd stock of Spain—
Her life, since Philip left her, and she lost
Her fierce desire of bearing him a child,
Hath, like a brief and bitter winter's day,
Gone narrowing down and darkening to a close.
There will be more conspiracies, I fear.

PAGET.

Ay, ay, beware of France.

HOWARD.

                O Paget, Paget!
I have seen heretics of the poorer sort,
Expectant of the rack from day to day,
To whom the fire were welcome, lying chain'd
In breathless dungeons over steaming sewers,
Fed with rank bread that crawl'd upon the
       tongue,
And putrid water, every drop a worm,

Until they died of rotted limbs; and then
Cast on the dunghill naked, and become
Hideously alive again from head to heel,
Made even the carrion-nosing mongrel vomit
With hate and horror.

PAGET.

        Nay, you sicken *me*
To hear you.

HOWARD.

        Fancy-sick; these things are done,
Done right against the promise of this Queen
Twice given.

PAGET.

        No faith with heretics, my Lord!
Hist! there be two old gossips — gospellers,
I take it; stand behind the pillar here;
I warrant you they talk about the burning.

Enter TWO OLD WOMEN.   JOAN, *and after her*
TIB.

JOAN.

Why, it be Tib!

TIB.

I cum behind tha, gall, and could n't make
tha hear.   Eh, the wind and the wet!   What a
day, what a day! nigh upo' judgement daay
loike.   Pwoaps be pretty things, Joan, but they
wunt set i' the Lord's cheer o' that daay.

JOAN.

I must set down myself, Tib; it be a var waay
vor my owld legs up vro' Islip. Eh, my rheu-
matizy be that bad howiver be I to win to the
burnin'.

TIB.

I should saay 't wur ower by now. I 'd ha'
been here avore, but Dumble wur blow'd wi' the
wind, and Dumble 's the best milcher in Islip.

JOAN.

Our Daisy 's as good 'z her.

TIB.

Noa, Joan.

JOAN.

Our Daisy's butter 's as good 'z hern.

TIB.

Noa, Joan.

JOAN.

Our Daisy's cheeses be better.

TIB.

Noa, Joan.

JOAN.

Eh, then ha' thy waay wi' me, Tib; ez thou hast wi' thy owld man.

TIB.

Ay, Joan, and my owld man wur up and awaay betimes wi' dree hard eggs for a good pleace at the burnin'; and barrin' the wet, Hodge 'ud ha' been a-harrowin' o' white peasen i' the outfield — and barrin' the wind, Dumble wur blow'd wi' the wind, so 'z we was forced to stick her, but we fetched her round at last. Thank the Lord therevore. Dumble 's the best milcher in Islip.

JOAN.

Thou 's thy way wi' man and beast, Tib. I wonder at tha, it beats me! Eh, but I do know ez Pwoaps and vires be bad things; tell 'ee now,

I heerd summat as summun towld summun o'
owld Bishop Gardiner's end; there wur an owld
lord a-cum to dine wi' un, and a wur so owld a
could n't bide vor his dinner, but a had to bide
howsomiver, vor 'I wunt dine,' says my Lord
Bishop, says he, 'not till I hears ez Latimer and
Ridley be a-vire;' and so they bided on and on
till vour o' the clock, till his man cum in post
vro' here, and tells un ez the vire has tuk holt.
'Now,' says the Bishop, says he, 'we 'll gwo to
dinner;' and the owld lord fell to 's meat wi' a
will, God bless un! but Gardiner wur struck
down like by the hand o' God avore a could
taste a mossel, and a set un all a-vire, so 'z the
tongue on un cum a-lolluping out o' 'is mouth
as black as a rat.   Thank the Lord therevore.

PAGET.

The fools!

TIB.

Ay, Joan; and Queen Mary gwoes on a-
burnin' and a-burnin', to get her baaby born;
but all her burnin's 'ill never burn out the
hypocrisy that makes the water in her.   There 's

nought but the vire of God's hell ez can burn
out that.

JOAN.

Thank the Lord therevore.

PAGET.

The fools!

TIB.

A-burnin', and a-burnin', and a-makin' o' volk
madder and madder; but tek thou my word
vor 't, Joan, — and I bean't wrong not twice i'
ten year — the burnin' o' the owld archbishop 'll
burn the Pwoap out o' this 'ere land vor iver
and iver.

HOWARD.

Out of the church, you brace of cursed crones,
Or I will have you duck'd!   (*Women hurry
     out.*)   Said I not right?
For how should reverend prelate or throned
     prince
Brook for an hour such brute malignity?
Ah, what an acrid wine has Luther brew'd!

PAGET.

Pooh, pooh, my Lord! poor garrulous country-
     wives.

Buy you their cheeses, and they 'll side with you;
You cannot judge the liquor from the lees.

HOWARD.

I think that in some sort we may.   But see,

(*Enter* PETERS.)

Peters, my gentleman, an honest Catholic,
Who follow'd with the crowd to Cranmer's fire.
One that would neither misreport nor lie,
Not to gain paradise: no, nor if the Pope
Charged him to do it— he is white as death.
Peters, how pale you look! you bring the smoke
Of Cranmer's burning with you.

PETERS.

Twice or thrice
The smoke of Cranmer's burning wrapt me
round.

HOWARD.

Peters, you know me Catholic, but English.
Did he die bravely?   Tell me that, or leave
All else untold.

PETERS.

My Lord, he died most bravely.

HOWARD.

Then tell me all.

PAGET.

Ay, Master Peters, tell us.

PETERS.

You saw him how he past among the crowd;
And ever as he walk'd the Spanish friars
Still plied him with entreaty and reproach:
But Cranmer, as the helmsman at the helm
Steers, ever looking to the happy haven
Where he shall rest at night, moved to his death;
And I could see that many silent hands
Came from the crowd and met his own; and
       thus,
When we had come where Ridley burnt with
       Latimer,
He, with a cheerful smile, as one whose mind
Is all made up, in haste put off the rags
They had mock'd his misery with, and all in
       white,
His long white beard, which he had never shaven
Since Henry's death, down-sweeping to the
       chain

Wherewith they bound him to the stake, he
    stood
More like an ancient father of the Church
Than heretic of these times; and still the friars
Plied him, but Cranmer only shook his head,
Or answer'd them in smiling negatives;
Whereat Lord Williams gave a sudden cry: —
' Make short! make short!' and so they lit the
    wood.
Then Cranmer lifted his left hand to heaven,
And thrust his right into the bitter flame;
And crying, in his deep voice, more than
    once,
' This hath offended — this unworthy hand!'
So held it till it all was burn'd, before
The flame had reach'd his body; I stood near —
Mark'd him — he never uttered moan of pain:
He never stirr'd or writhed, but, like a statue,
Unmoving in the greatness of the flame,
Gave up the ghost; and so past martyr-like —
Martyr I may not call him — past — but whither?

PAGET.

To purgatory, man, to purgatory.

PETERS.

Nay, but, my Lord, he denied purgatory.

PAGET.

Why then to heaven, and God ha' mercy on him.

HOWARD.

Paget, despite his fearful heresies,
I loved the man, and needs must moan for him;
O Cranmer!
                    PAGET.
          But your moan is useless now:
Come out, my Lord, it is a world of fools.

                                        [*Exeunt.*

ACT V.

SCENE I.— London. Hall in the Palace.

Queen, Sir Nicholas Heath.

Heath.

Madam,
I do assure you that it must be look'd to :
Calais is but ill-garrison'd, in Guisnes
Are scarce two hundred men, and the French
     fleet
Rule in the narrow seas. It must be look'd to,
If war should fall between yourself and France ;
Or you will lose your Calais.

Mary.

            It shall be look'd to ;
I wish you a good morning, good Sir Nicholas :
Here is the King.   [*Exit* Heath.

Enter PHILIP.

PHILIP.

       Sir Nicholas tells you true,
And you must look to Calais when I go.

MARY.

Go? must you go, indeed — again — so soon?
Why, nature's licensed vagabond, the swallow,
That might live always in the sun's warm heart,
Stays longer here in our poor north than you —
Knows where he nested — ever comes again.

PHILIP.

And, Madam, so shall I.

MARY.

           Oh, will you? will you?
I am faint with fear that you will come no more.

PHILIP.

Ay, ay; but many voices call me hence.

MARY.

Voices — I hear unhappy rumours — nay,
I say not, I believe.   What voices call you

Dearer than mine that should be dearest to you?
Alas, my Lord! what voices and how many?

PHILIP.

The voices of Castile and Aragon,
Granada, Naples, Sicily, and Milan,—
The voices of Franche-Comté, and the Nether-
      lands,
The voices of Peru and Mexico,
Tunis, and Oran, and the Philippines,
And all the fair spice-islands of the East.

MARY (*admiringly*).

You are the mightiest monarch upon earth,
I but a little Queen: and so, indeed,
Need you the more.

PHILIP.

                    A little Queen! but when
I came to wed your majesty, Lord Howard,
Sending an insolent shot that dash'd the seas
Upon us, made us lower our kingly flag
To yours of England.

MARY.

Howard is all English!
There is no king, not were he ten times king,
Ten times our husband, but must lower his flag
To that of England in the seas of England.

PHILIP.

Is that your answer?

MARY.

Being Queen of England,
I have none other.

PHILIP.
So.

MARY.

But wherefore not
Helm the huge vessel of your state, my liege,
Here by the side of her who loves you most?

PHILIP.

No, Madam, no! a candle in the sun
Is all but smoke — a star beside the moon
Is all but lost; your people will not crown me —

Your people are as cheerless as your clime;
Hate me and mine: witness the brawls, the
      gibbets.
Here swings a Spaniard — there an Englishman;
The peoples are unlike as their complexion;
Yet will I be your swallow and return —
But now I cannot bide.

MARY.

          Not to help *me?*
They hate *me* also for my love to you,
My Philip; and these judgments on the land —
Harvestless autumns, horrible agues, plague —

PHILIP.

The blood and sweat of heretics at the stake
Is God's best dew upon the barren field.
Burn more!

MARY.

      I will, I will; and you will stay?

PHILIP.

Have I not said?   Madam, I came to sue
Your Council and yourself to declare **war.**

MARY.

Sir, there are many English in your ranks
To help your battle.

PHILIP.

So far, good.   I say
I came to sue your Council and yourself
To declare war against the King of France.

MARY.

Not to see me?

PHILIP.

Ay, Madam, to see you.
Unalterably and pesteringly fond!   [*Aside.*
But soon or late you must have war with
          France;
King Henry warms your traitors at his hearth.
Carew is there, and Thomas Stafford there.
Courtenay, belike —

MARY.

A fool and featherhead!

PHILIP.

Ay, but they use his name.   In brief, this Henry
Stirs up your land against you to the intent

That you may lose your English heritage.
And then, your Scottish namesake marrying
The Dauphin, he would weld France, England,
         Scotland,
Into one sword to hack at Spain and me.

MARY.

And yet the Pope is now colleagued with
         France;
You make your wars upon him down in Italy: —
Philip, can that be well?

PHILIP.

                    Content you, Madam;
You must abide my judgement, and my father's,
Who deems it a most just and holy war.
The Pope would cast the Spaniard out of Naples:
He calls us worse than Jews, Moors, Saracens.
The Pope has pushed his horns beyond his
         mitre —
Beyond his province.   Now,
Duke Alva will but touch him on the horns,
And he withdraws; and of his holy head —
For Alva is true son of the true church —
No hair is harm'd.   Will you not help me here?

MARY.

Alas! the Council will not hear of war.

They say your wars are not the wars of England.

They will not lay more taxes on a land

So hunger-nipt and wretched; and you know

The crown is poor.   We have given the church-
       lands back:

The nobles would not; nay, they clapt their
       hands

Upon their swords when ask'd; and therefore
       God

Is hard upon the people.   What's to be done?

Sir, I will move them in your cause again,

And we will raise us loans and subsidies

Among the merchants; and Sir Thomas Gresham

Will aid us.   There is Antwerp and the Jews.

PHILIP.

Madam, my thanks.

MARY.

             And you will stay your going?

PHILIP.

And further to discourage and lay lame

The plots of France, altho' you love her not,

You must proclaim Elizabeth your heir.
She stands between you and the Queen of Scots.

MARY.

The Queen of Scots at least is Catholic.

PHILIP.

Ay, Madam, Catholic; but I will not have
The King of France the King of England too.

MARY.

But she's a heretic, and, when I am gone,
Brings the new learning back.

PHILIP.

      It must be done.
You must proclaim Elizabeth your heir.

MARY.

Then it is done; but you will stay your going
Somewhat beyond your settled purpose?

PHILIP.

        No!

MARY.

What, not one day?

PHILIP.

You beat upon the rock.

MARY.

And I am broken there.

PHILIP.

Is this a place
To wail in, Madam? what! a public hall?
Go in, I pray you.

MARY.

Do not seem so changed.
Say go; but only say it lovingly.

PHILIP.

You do mistake.   I am not one to change.
I never loved you more.

MARY.

Sire, I obey you.
Come quickly.

PHILIP.

Ay.   [*Exit* MARY.

Enter COUNT DE FERIA.

FERIA (*aside*).

The Queen in tears!

PHILIP.

Feria!

Hast thou not mark'd — come closer to mine
    ear —
How doubly aged this Queen of ours hath grown
Since she lost hope of bearing us a child?

FERIA.

Sire, if your Grace hath mark'd it, so have I.

PHILIP.

Hast thou not likewise mark'd Elizabeth,
How fair and royal — like a Queen, indeed?

FERIA.

Allow me the same answer as before —
That if your Grace hath mark'd her, so have I.

PHILIP.

Good, now; methinks my Queen is like enough
To leave me by and by.

FERIA.

To leave you, sire?

PHILIP.

I mean not like to live.   Elizabeth —
To Philibert of Savoy, as you know,
We meant to wed her; but I am not sure
She will not serve me better — so my Queen
Would leave me — as — my wife.

FERIA.

                              Sire, even so.

PHILIP.

She will not have Prince Philibert of Savoy.

FERIA.

No, sire.

PHILIP.

        I have to pray you, some odd time,
To sound the Princess carelessly on this;
Not as from me, but as your phantasy;
And tell me how she takes it.

FERIA.

                              Sire, I will.

PHILIP.

I am not certain but that Philibert
Shall be the man; and I shall urge his suit

Upon the Queen, because I am not certain:
You understand, Feria.

FERIA.
Sire, I do.

PHILIP.
And if you be not secret in this matter,
You understand me there, too?

FERIA.
Sire, I do.

PHILIP.
You must be sweet and supple, like a French-
    man.
She is none of those who loathe the honeycomb.

[*Exit* FERIA.

Enter RENARD.

RENARD.
My liege, I bring you goodly tidings.

PHILIP.
Well?

RENARD.
There *will* be war with France, at last, my liege;
Sir Thomas Stafford, a bull-headed ass,

Sailing from France, with thirty Englishmen,
Hath taken Scarboro' Castle, north of York;
Proclaims himself protector, and affirms
The Queen has forfeited her right to reign
By marriage with an alien — other things
As idle; a weak Wyatt!   Little doubt
This buzz will soon be silenced; but the Council
(I have talk'd with some already) are for war.
This is the fifth conspiracy hatch'd in France;
They show their teeth upon it; and your Grace,
So you will take advice of mine, should stay
Yet for a while, to shape and guide the event.

PHILIP.

Good! Renard, I will stay then.

RENARD.

                              Also, sire,
Might I not say — to please your wife, the
          Queen?
                    PHILIP.
Ay, Renard, if you care to put it so.

                              [*Exeunt.*

SCENE II. — A Room in the Palace.

Mary, *sitting : a rose in her hand.* Lady Clarence. Alice *in the background.*

MARY.

Look! I have play'd with this poor rose so long
I have broken off the head.

LADY CLARENCE.

Your Grace hath been
More merciful to many a rebel head
That should have fallen, and may rise again.

MARY.

There were not many hang'd for Wyatt's rising.

LADY CLARENCE.

Nay, not two hundred.

MARY.

I could weep for them
And her, and mine own self and all the world.

LADY CLARENCE.

For her? for whom, your Grace?

Enter USHER.

USHER.
The Cardinal.

Enter CARDINAL POLE.   (MARY *rises.*)

MARY.

Reginald Pole, what news hath plagued thy
heart?
What makes thy favour like the bloodless head
Fallen on the block, and held up by the hair?
Philip? —

POLE.

No, Philip is as warm in life
As ever.

MARY.

Ay, and then as cold as ever.
Is Calais taken?

POLE.

Cousin, there hath chanced
A sharper harm to England and to Rome
Than Calais taken.   Julius the Third
Was ever just, and mild, and father-like ;
But this new Pope Caraffa, Paul the Fourth,
Not only reft me of that legateship

Which Julius gave me, and the legateship
Annex'd to Canterbury — nay, but worse —
And yet I must obey the Holy Father,
And so must you, good cousin ;— worse than all,
A passing bell toll'd in a dying ear —
He hath cited me to Rome, for heresy,
Before his Inquisition.

MARY.

I knew it, cousin,
But held from you all papers sent by Rome,
That you might rest among us, till the Pope,
To compass which I wrote myself to Rome,
Reversed his doom, and that you might not
    seem
To disobey his Holiness.

POLE.

He hates Philip ;
He is all Italian, and he hates the Spaniard ;
He cannot dream that *I* advised the war ;
He strikes thro' me at Philip and yourself.
Nay, but I know it of old, he hates me too ;
So brands me in the stare of Christendom
A heretic !

VOL. XI. — 17

Now, even now, when bow'd before my time,
The house half-ruin'd ere the lease be out;
When I should guide the Church in peace at
         home,
After my twenty years of banishment,
And all my lifelong labour to uphold
The primacy — a heretic!   Long ago,
When I was ruler in the patrimony,
I was too lenient to the Lutheran,
And I and learned friends among ourselves
Would freely canvass certain Lutheranisms.
What then, he knew I was no Lutheran.
A heretic!
He drew this shaft against me to the head,
When it was thought I might be chosen Pope,
But then withdrew it.   In full consistory,
When I was made Archbishop, he approved me.
And how should he have sent me Legate hither,
Deeming me heretic? and what heresy since?
But he was evermore mine enemy,
And hates the Spaniard — fiery-choleric,
A drinker of black, strong, volcanic wines,
That ever make him fierier.   I, a heretic?

Your Highness knows that in pursuing heresy
I have gone beyond your late Lord Chancellor, —
He cried Enough! enough! before his death, —
Gone beyond him and mine own natural man
(It was God's cause); so far they call me now,
The scourge and butcher of their English church.

MARY.

Have courage, your reward is heaven itself.

POLE.

They groan amen; they swarm into the fire
Like flies — for what? no dogma. They know
        nothing;
They burn for nothing.

MARY.

            You have done your best.

POLE.

Have done my best, and as a faithful son,
That all day long hath wrought his father's work,
When back he comes at evening hath the door
Shut on him by the father whom he loved,
His early follies cast into his teeth,

And the poor son turn'd out into the street
To sleep, to die — I shall die of it, cousin.

MARY.

I pray you be not so disconsolate;
I still will do mine utmost with the Pope.
Poor cousin!
Have not I been the fast friend of your life
Since mine began, and it was thought we two
Might make one flesh, and cleave unto each
        other
As man and wife?

POLE.

                    Ah, cousin, I remember
How I would dandle you upon my knee
At lisping-age.   I watch'd you dancing once
With your huge father; he look'd the Great
        Harry,
You but his cockboat; prettily you did it,
And innocently.   No — we were not made
One flesh in happiness, no happiness here;
But now we are made one flesh in misery;
Our bridemaids are not lovely — Disappoint-
        ment,

Ingratitude, Injustice, Evil-tongue,
Labour-in-vain.

MARY.

Surely, not all in vain.
Peace, cousin, peace! I am sad at heart myself.

POLE.

Our altar is a mound of dead men's clay,
Dug from the grave that yawns for us beyond;
And there is one Death stands behind the
    Groom,
And there is one Death stands behind the
    Bride —

MARY.

Have you been looking at the 'Dance of Death'?

POLE.

No; but these libellous papers which I found
Strewn in your palace. Look you here — the
    Pope
Pointing at me with ' Pole, the heretic,
Thou hast burnt others, do thou burn thyself,
Or I will burn thee; ' and this other; see! —
'We pray continually for the death

Of our accursed Queen and Cardinal Pole.'
This last — I dare not read it her.   [*Aside.*

MARY.

               Away!
Why do you bring me these?
I thought you knew me better.   I never read,
I tear them; they come back upon my dreams.
The hands that write them should be burnt
      clean off
As Cranmer's, and the fiends that utter them
Tongue-torn with pincers, lash'd to death, or lie
Famishing in black cells, while famish'd rats
Eat them alive.   Why do they bring me these?
Do you mean to drive me mad?

POLE.

              I had forgotten
How these poor libels trouble you.   Your pardon,
Sweet cousin, and farewell!   ' O bubble world,
Whose colours in a moment break and fly!'
Why, who said that?   I know not — true enough!
    [*Puts up the papers, all but the last, which
       falls.   Exit* POLE.

ALICE.

If Cranmer's spirit were a mocking one,
And heard these two, there might be sport for
    him.   [*Aside.*

MARY.

Clarence, they hate me; even while I speak
There lurks a silent dagger, listening
In some dark closet, some long gallery, drawn,
And panting for my blood as I go by.

LADY CLARENCE.

Nay, Madam, there be loyal papers too,
And I have often found them.

MARY.

                Find me one!

LADY CLARENCE.

Ay, Madam; but Sir Nicholas Heath, the Chan-
    cellor,
Would see your Highness.

MARY.

          Wherefore should I see him?

LADY CLARENCE.

Well, Madam, he may bring you news from
    Philip.

MARY.

So, Clarence.

LADY CLARENCE.

                Let me first put up your hair;
It tumbles all abroad.

MARY.

                    And the gray dawn
Of an old age that never will be mine
Is all the clearer seen.   No, no; what matters?
Forlorn I am, and let me look forlorn.

Enter SIR NICHOLAS HEATH.

HEATH.

I bring your Majesty such grievous news
I grieve to bring it.   Madam, Calais is taken.

MARY.

What traitor spoke?   Here, let my cousin Pole
Seize him and burn him for a Lutheran.

HEATH.

Her Highness is unwell.   I will retire.

LADY CLARENCE.

Madam, your Chancellor, Sir Nicholas Heath.

MARY.

Sir Nicholas! I am stunn'd — Nicholas Heath?
Methought some traitor smote me on the head.
What said you, my good Lord, that our brave
        English
Had sallied out from Calais and driven back
The Frenchmen from their trenches?

HEATH.

                    Alas! no.
That gateway to the mainland over which
Our flag hath floated for two hundred years
Is France again.

MARY.

            So; but it is not lost —
Not yet.   Send out: let England as of old
Rise lionlike, strike hard and deep into
The prey they are rending from her — ay, and
        rend
The renders too.   Send out, send out, and make
Musters in all the counties; gather all

From sixteen years to sixty; collect the fleet;
Let every craft that carries sail and gun
Steer toward Calais.   Guisnes is not taken yet?

HEATH.

Guisnes is not taken yet.

MARY.

There yet is hope.

HEATH.

Ah, Madam, but your people are so cold;
I do much fear that England will not care.
Methinks there is no manhood left among us.

MARY.

Send out; I am too weak to stir abroad:
Tell my mind to the Council — to the Parlia-
        ment:
Proclaim it to the winds.   Thou art cold thyself
To babble of their coldness. Oh, would I were
My father for an hour!   Away now — quick!
                              [*Exit* HEATH.
I hoped I had served God with all my might!
It seems I have not.   Ah! much heresy

Shelter'd in Calais.   Saints, I have rebuilt
Your shrines, set up your broken images;
Be comfortable to me.   Suffer not
That my brief reign in England be defamed
Thro' all her angry chronicles hereafter
By loss of Calais.   Grant me Calais.   Philip,
We have made war upon the Holy Father
All for your sake: what good could come of
        that?

LADY CLARENCE.

No, Madam, not against the Holy Father;
You did but help King Philip's war with France,
Your troops were never down in Italy.

MARY.

I am a byword.   Heretic and rebel
Point at me and make merry.   Philip gone!
And Calais gone!   Time that I were gone too!

LADY CLARENCE.

Nay, if the fetid gutter had a voice
And cried I was not clean, what should I care?
Or you, for heretic cries?   And I believe,
Spite of your melancholy Sir Nicholas,
Your England is as loyal as myself.

MARY (*seeing the paper dropt by* POLE).
There! there! another paper! Said you not
Many of these were loyal? Shall I try
If this be one of such?

LADY CLARENCE.

        Let it be, let it be.
God pardon me! I have never yet found one.
                    [*Aside.*

MARY (*reads*).

' Your people hate you as your husband hates
    you.'
Clarence, Clarence, what have I done? what sin
Beyond all grace, all pardon? Mother of God,
Thou knowest never woman meant so well,
And fared so ill in this disastrous world.
My people hate me and desire my death.

LADY CLARENCE.

No, Madam, no.

MARY.

My husband hates me, and desires my death.

LADY CLARENCE.

No, Madam ; these are libels.

MARY.

I hate myself, and I desire my death.

LADY CLARENCE.

Long live your Majesty ! Shall Alice sing you
One of her pleasant songs?   Alice, my child,
Bring us your lute (ALICE *goes*). They say the
        gloom of Saul
Was lighten'd by young David's harp.

MARY.

                                  Too young !
And never knew a Philip.

Re-enter ALICE.

                          Give *me* the lute.
He hates me !
                (She sings.)

Hapless doom of woman happy in betrothing !
Beauty passes like a breath, and love is lost in loathing :
Low, my lute ; speak low, my lute, but say the world is
      nothing —
                Low, lute, low !
Love will hover round the flowers when they first awaken ;
Love will fly the fallen leaf, and not be overtaken ;
Low, my lute ! oh, low, my lute ! we fade and are forsaken —
                Low, dear lute, low !

Take it away ! not low enough for me !

ALICE.

Your Grace hath a low voice.

MARY.

                    How daré you say it?

Even for that he hates me.   A low voice
Lost in a wilderness where none can hear!
A voice of shipwreck on a shoreless sea!
A low voice from the dust and from the grave!
(*Sitting on the ground*).   There, am I low
     enough now?

ALICE.

Good Lord! how grim and ghastly looks her
     Grace,
With both her knees drawn upward to her chin.
There was an old-world tomb beside my father's,
And this was open'd, and the dead were found
Sitting, and in this fashion; she looks a corpse.

Enter LADY MAGDALEN DACRES.

LADY MAGDALEN.

Madam, the Count de Feria waits without,
In hopes to see your Highness.

LADY CLARENCE (*pointing to* MARY).

                          Wait he must —

Her trance again.   She neither sees nor hears,

And may not speak for hours.

LADY MAGDALEN.

                          Unhappiest

Of queens and wives and women!

ALICE (*in the foreground with* LADY MAG-
DALEN).

                          And all along

Of Philip.

LADY MAGDALEN.

                  Not so loud! Our Clarence there

Sees ever such an aureole round the Queen,

It gilds the greatest wronger of her peace,

Who stands the nearest to her.

ALICE.

                       Ay, this Philip;

I used to love the Queen with all my heart —

God help me, but methinks I love her less

For such a dotage upon such a man.

I would I were as tall and strong as you.

LADY MAGDALEN.
I seem half-shamed at times to be so tall.

ALICE.
You are the stateliest deer in all the herd —
Beyond his aim — but I am small and scandalous,
And love to hear bad tales of Philip.

LADY MAGDALEN.
       Why?
I never heard him utter worse of you
Than that you were low-statured.

ALICE.
      Does he think
Low stature is low nature, or all women's
Low as his own?

LADY MAGDALEN.
     There you strike in the nail.
This coarseness is a want of phantasy.
It is the low man thinks the woman low;
Sin is too dull to see beyond himself.

ALICE.
Ah, Magdalen, sin is bold as well as dull.
How dared he?

LADY MAGDALEN.

      Stupid soldiers oft are bold.
Poor lads, they see not what the general sees,
A risk of utter ruin. I am *not*
Beyond his aim, or was not.

ALICE.

          Who? Not you?
Tell, tell me; save my credit with myself.

LADY MAGDALEN.

I never breathed it to a bird in the eaves,
Would not for all the stars and maiden moon
Our drooping Queen should know! In Hampton
      Court
My window look'd upon the corridor;
And I was robing; — this poor throat of mine
Barer than I should wish a man to see it, —
When he we speak of drove the window back,
And, like a thief, push'd in his royal hand;
But by God's providence a good stout staff
Lay near me, and you know me strong of arm:
I do believe I lamed his Majesty's
For a day or two, tho', give the devil his due,
I never found he bore me any spite.
    VOL. XI.— 18

ALICE.

I would she could have wedded that poor youth,
My Lord of Devon, — light enough, God knows,
And mixt with Wyatt's rising, — and the boy
Not out of him — but neither cold, coarse, cruel,
And more than all — no Spaniard.

LADY CLARENCE.

Not so loud.
Lord Devon, girls! what are you whispering
  here?

ALICE.

Probing an old state-secret — how it chanced
That this young Earl was sent on foreign travel,
Not lost his head.

LADY CLARENCE.

There was no proof against him.

ALICE.

Nay, Madam; did not Gardiner intercept
A letter which the Count de Noailles wrote
To that dead traitor Wyatt, with full proof
Of Courtenay's treason? What became of that?

LADY CLARENCE.

Some say that Gardiner, out of love for him,
Burnt it, and some relate that it was lost
When Wyatt sack'd the Chancellor's house in
      Southwark.
Let dead things rest.

ALICE.
            Ay, and with him who died
Alone in Italy.

LADY CLARENCE.
            Much changed, I hear,
Had put off levity and put graveness on.
The foreign courts report him in his manner
Noble as his young person and old shield.
It might be so — but all is over now;
He caught a chill in the lagoons of Venice,
And died in Padua.

MARY (*looking up suddenly*).
            Died in the true faith?

LADY CLARENCE.
Ay, Madam, happily.

MARY.

Happier he than I.

LADY MAGDALEN.

It seems her Highness hath awaken'd. Think
        you
That I might dare to tell her that the Count —

MARY.

I will see no man hence for evermore,
Saving my confessor and my cousin Pole.

LADY MAGDALEN.

It is the Count de Feria, my dear lady.

MARY.

What Count?

LADY MAGDALEN.

The Count de Feria, from his Majesty
King Philip.

MARY.

            Philip! quick! loop up my hair!
Throw cushions on that seat, and make it throne-
        like.
Arrange my dress — the gorgeous Indian shawl
That Philip brought me in our happy days! —

That covers all. So — am I somewhat queen-
    like,
Bride of the mightiest sovereign upon earth?

LADY CLARENCE.
Ay, so your Grace would bide a moment yet.

MARY.
No, no, he brings a letter.   I may die
Before I read it.   Let me see him at once.

Enter COUNT DE FERIA (*kneels*).

FERIA.
I trust your Grace is well.   (*Aside.*) How her
    hand burns!

MARY.
I am not well, but it will better me,
Sir Count, to read the letter which you bring.

FERIA.
Madam, I bring no letter.

MARY.
                    How! no letter?

FERIA.

His Highness is so vex'd with strange affairs —

MARY.

That his own wife is no affair of his.

FERIA.

Nay, Madam, nay! he sends his veriest love,
And says he will come quickly.

MARY.

              Doth he, indeed?
You, sir, do *you* remember what *you* said
When last you came to England?

FERIA.

              Madam, I brought
My King's congratulations; it was hoped
Your Highness was once more in happy state
To give him an heir male.

MARY.

              Sir, you said more;
You said he would come quickly. I had horses
On all the road from Dover, day and night;
On all the road from Harwich, night and day;

But the child came not, and the husband came
      not;
And yet he will come quickly. . . . Thou hast
      learnt
Thy lesson, and I mine.   There is no need
For Philip so to shame himself again.
Return,
And tell him that I know he comes no more.
Tell him at last I know his love is dead,
And that I am in state to bring forth death —
Thou art commission'd to Elizabeth,
And not to me!

FERIA.

             Mere compliments and wishes.
But shall I take some message from your Grace?

MARY.

Tell her to come and close my dying eyes,
And wear my crown, and dance upon my grave.

FERIA.

Then I may say your Grace will see your sister?
Your Grace is too low-spirited.   Air and sun-
      shine.

I would we had you, Madam, in our warm Spain.
You droop in your dim London.

MARY.
                              Have him away!
I sicken of his readiness.

LADY CLARENCE.
                              My Lord Count,
Her Highness is too ill for colloquy.

FERIA (*kneels, and kisses her hand*).
I wish her Highness better. (*Aside.*) How her
      hand burns!   [*Exeunt.*

SCENE III. — A House near London.

ELIZABETH, STEWARD OF THE HOUSEHOLD, ATTENDANTS.

ELIZABETH.
There 's half an angel wrong'd in your account;
Methinks I am all angel, that I bear it
Without more ruffling.   Cast it o'er again.

STEWARD.
I were whole devil if I wrong'd you, Madam.
                              [*Exit* STEWARD.

QUEEN MARY.

ATTENDANT.

The Count de Feria, from the King of Spain.

ELIZABETH.

Ah! — let him enter.   Nay, you need not go:

[*To her* LADIES.

Remain within the chamber, but apart.

We'll have no private conference.   Welcome to
England!

Enter FERIA.

FERIA.

Fair island star!

ELIZABETH.

I shine! What else, Sir Count?

FERIA.

As far as France, and into Philip's heart.

My King would know if you be fairly served,

And lodged, and treated.

ELIZABETH.

You see the lodging, sir,

I am well-served, and am in everything

Most loyal and most grateful to the Queen.

FERIA.

You should be grateful to my master, too.
He spoke of this; and unto him you owe
That Mary hath acknowledged you her heir.

ELIZABETH.

No, not to her nor him; but to the people,
Who know my right, and love me, as I love
The people! whom God aid!

FERIA.

                              You will be Queen,
And, were I Philip —

ELIZABETH.

              Wherefore pause you — what?

FERIA.

Nay, but I speak from mine own self, not him,
Your royal sister cannot last; your hand
Will be much coveted! What a delicate one!
Our Spanish ladies have none such — and there,
Were you in Spain, this fine fair gossamer
          gold —
Like sun-gilt breathings on a frosty dawn —
That hovers round your shoulder —

ELIZABETH.

Is it so fine?

Troth, some have said so.

FERIA.

— would be deemed a miracle.

ELIZABETH.

Your Philip hath gold hair and golden beard;
There must be ladies many with hair like mine.

FERIA.

Some few of Gothic blood have golden hair,
But none like yours.

ELIZABETH.

I am happy you approve it.

FERIA.

But as to Philip and your Grace, — consider, —
If such a one as you should match with Spain,
What hinders but that Spain and England join'd
Should make the mightiest empire earth has
known.
Spain would be England on her seas, and Eng-
land
Mistress of the Indies.

ELIZABETH.

It may chance that England
Will be the Mistress of the Indies yet,
Without the help of Spain.

FERIA.

Impossible;
Except you put Spain down.
Wide of the mark even for a madman's dream.

ELIZABETH.

Perhaps; but we have seamen. Count de Feria,
I take it that the King hath spoken to you;
But is Don Carlos such a goodly match?

FERIA.

Don Carlos, Madam, is but twelve years old.

ELIZABETH.

Ay, tell the King that I will muse upon it;
He is my good friend, and I would keep him so;
But — he would have me Catholic of Rome,
And that I scarce can be; and, sir, till now
My sister's marriage, and my father's marriages,
Make me full fain to live and die a maid.

But I am much beholden to your King.
Have you aught else to tell me?

FERIA.

                        Nothing, Madam,
Save that methought I gather'd from the Queen
That she would see your Grace before she —
        died.
ELIZABETH.

God's death! and wherefore spake you not
        before?
We dally with our lazy moments here,
And hers are number'd.   Horses there, without!
I am much beholden to the King, your master.
Why did you keep me prating?   Horses, there!
            [*Exit* ELIZABETH, *etc.*

FERIA.

So from a clear sky falls the thunderbolt!
Don Carlos?   Madam, if you marry Philip,
Then I and he will snaffle your 'God's death,'
And break your paces in, and make you tame;
God's death, forsooth — you do not know King
        Philip!   [*Exit.*

SCENE IV. — London.   Before the Palace.

A light burning within. Voices *of the night passing.*

First.

Is not yon light in the Queen's chamber?

Second.
                                               Ay,
They say she 's dying.

First.
                        So is Cardinal Pole.
May the great angels join their wings, and make
Down for their heads to heaven!

Second.
                          Amen.   Come on.
                                 [*Exeunt.*
Two Others.

First.

There 's the Queen's light.   I hear she cannot
  live.

Second.

God curse her and her Legate!   Gardiner burns
Already; but to pay them full in kind,
The hottest hold in all the devil's den
Were but a sort of winter; sir, in Guernsey,
I watch'd a woman burn; and in her agony
The mother came upon her — a child was born —
And, sir, they hurl'd it back into the fire,
That, being but baptized in fire, the babe
Might be in fire for ever.   Ah, good neighbour,
There should be something fierier than fire
To yield them their deserts.

First.

Amen to all
Your wish, and further!

A Third Voice.

Deserts!   Amen to what?   Whose deserts?
Yours?   You have a gold ring on your finger,
and soft raiment about your body; and is not
the woman up yonder sleeping after all she has
done, in peace and quietness, on a soft bed, in a
closed room, with light, fire, physic, tendance;

and I have seen the true men of Christ lying
famine-dead by scores, and under no ceiling but
the cloud that wept on them, not for them.

FIRST.

Friend, tho' so late, it is not safe to preach.
You had best go home.   What are you?

THIRD.

What am I?   One who cries continually with
sweat and tears to the Lord God that it would
please Him out of His infinite love to break
down all kingship and queenship, all priesthood
and prelacy; to cancel and abolish all bonds of
human allegiance, all the magistracy, all the
nobles, and all the wealthy; and to send us
again, according to His promise, the one King,
the Christ, and all things in common, as in the
day of the first church, when Christ Jesus was
King.

FIRST.

If ever I heard a madman, — let's away!
Why, you long-winded —   Sir, you go beyond
         me.
I pride myself on being moderate.

Good night! Go home. Besides, you curse
    so loud
The watch will hear you. Get you home at
    once.   [*Exeunt.*

SCENE V.— LONDON.   A ROOM IN THE
PALACE.

*A Gallery on one side. The moonlight streaming
through a range of windows on the wall oppo-
site.* MARY, LADY CLARENCE, LADY MAG-
DALEN DACRES, ALICE. QUEEN *pacing the
Gallery. A writing-table in front.* QUEEN
*comes to the table and writes and goes again,
pacing the Gallery.*

LADY CLARENCE.

Mine eyes are dim: what hath she written? read.

ALICE.

'I am dying, Philip; come to me.'

LADY MAGDALEN.

There — up and down, poor lady, up and down.

ALICE.

And how her shadow crosses one by one
The moonlight casements pattern'd on the wall,
Following her like her sorrow!   She turns again.
                [QUEEN *sits and writes, and goes again.*

LADY CLARENCE.

What hath she written now?

ALICE.

Nothing; but 'come, come, come,' and all awry,
And blotted by her tears.   This cannot last.
                            [QUEEN *returns.*

MARY.

I whistle to the bird has broken cage,
And all in vain.   [*Sitting down.*
Calais gone — Guisnes gone, too — and Philip
    gone!

LADY CLARENCE.

Dear Madam, Philip is but at the wars;
I cannot doubt but that he comes again;
And he is with you in a measure still.
I never look'd upon so fair a likeness

As your great King in armour there, his hand
Upon his helmet.

   [*Pointing to the portrait of* Philip *on the wall.*

Mary.

       Doth he not look noble?
I had heard of him in battle over seas,
And I would have my warrior all in arms.
He said it was not courtly to stand helmeted
Before the Queen.   He had his gracious moment,
Altho' you 'll not believe me.   How he smiles
As if he loved me yet!

Lady Clarence.

       And so he does.

Mary.

He never loved me — nay, he could not love me.
It was his father's policy against France.
I am eleven years older than he,
Poor boy!   [*Weeps.*

Alice.

That was a lusty boy of twenty-seven;   [*Aside.*
Poor enough in God's grace!

MARY.

And all in vain!
The Queen of Scots is married to the Dauphin,
And Charles, the lord of this low world, is gone;
And all his wars and wisdoms past away;
And in a moment I shall follow him.

LADY CLARENCE.
Nay, dearest Lady, see your good physician.

MARY.
Drugs — but he knows they cannot help me —
　　says
That rest is all — tells me I must not think —
That I must rest — I shall rest by and by.
Catch the wild cat, cage him, and when he springs
And maims himself against the bars, say 'rest':
Why, you must kill him if you would have him
　　rest —
Dead or alive, you cannot make him happy.

LADY CLARENCE.
Your Majesty has lived so pure a life,
And done such mighty things by Holy Church,
I trust that God will make you happy yet.

MARY.

What is the strange thing happiness?   Sit down
        here
Tell me thine happiest hour.

LADY CLARENCE.

                              I will, if that
May make your Grace forget yourself a little.
There runs a shallow brook across our field
For twenty miles, where the black crow flies
        five,
And doth so bound and babble all the way
As if itself were happy.   It was May-time,
And I was walking with the man I loved.
I loved him, but I thought I was not loved.
And both were silent, letting the wild brook
Speak for us — till he stoop'd and gather'd
        one
From out a bed of thick forget-me-nots,
Look'd hard and sweet at me, and gave it me.
I took it, tho' I did not know I took it,
And put it in my bosom, and all at once
I felt his arms about me, and his lips —

MARY.

O God! I have been too slack, too slack;

There are Hot Gospellers even among our
        guards —

Nobles we dared not touch.   We have but burnt

The heretic priest, workmen, and women and
        children.

Wet, famine, ague, fever, storm, wreck, wrath, —

We have so play'd the coward; but by God's
        grace,

We 'll follow Philip's leading, and set up

The Holy Office here — garner the wheat,

And burn the tares with unquenchable fire!

Burn ! —

Fie, what a savour! tell the cooks to close

The doors of all the offices below.

Latimer!

Sir, we are private with our women here —

Ever a rough, blunt, and uncourtly fellow —

Thou light a torch that never will go out!

'T is out — mine flames.   Women, the Holy
        Father

Has ta'en the legateship from our cousin Pole --

Was that well done? and poor Pole pines of it,
As I do, to the death. I am but a woman,
I have no power. — Ah, weak and meek old man,
Sevenfold dishonour'd even in the sight
Of thine own sectaries — No, no. No pardon ! —
Why, that was false: there is the right hand still
Beckons me hence.
Sir, you were burnt for heresy, not for treason,
Remember that! 't was I and Bonner did it,
And Pole; we are three to one — Have you
          found mercy there,
Grant it me here: and see, he smiles and goes,
Gentle as in life.

ALICE.

Madam, who goes?   King Philip?

MARY.

No, Philip comes and goes, but never goes.
Women, when I am dead,
Open my heart, and there you will find written
Two names, Philip and Calais; open his, —
So that he have one, —
You will find Philip only, policy, policy, —
Ay, worse than that — not one hour true to me !

Foul maggots crawling in a fester'd vice!
Adulterous to the very heart of hell!
Hast thou a knife?

ALICE.

Ay, Madam, but o' God's mercy —

MARY.

Fool, think'st thou I would peril mine own soul
By slaughter of the body? I could not, girl,
Not this way — callous with a constant stripe,
Unwoundable. The knife!

ALICE.

Take heed, take heed!
The blade is keen as death.

MARY.

This Philip shall not
Stare in upon me in my haggardness;
Old, miserable, diseased,
Incapable of children. Come thou down.
        [*Cuts out the picture and throws it down.*
Lie there. (*Wails.*) O God, I have kill'd my
        Philip!

ALICE.

No,

Madam, you have but cut the canvas out;
We can replace it.

MARY.

All is well then; rest —
I will to rest; he said I must have rest.

[*Cries of* ' ELIZABETH ' *in the street.*

A cry! What 's that? Elizabeth? revolt?
A new Northumberland, another Wyatt?
I 'll fight it on the threshold of the grave.

LADY CLARENCE.

Madam, your royal sister comes to see you.

MARY.

I will not see her.
Who knows if Boleyn's daughter be my sister?
I will see none except the priest. Your arm.

[*To* LADY CLARENCE.

O Saint of Aragon, with that sweet worn smile
Among thy patient wrinkles — help me hence.

[*Exeunt.*

The Priest *passes.   Enter* Elizabeth *and* Sir
William Cecil.

Elizabeth.

Good counsel yours. — No one in waiting ? still,
As if the chamberlain were Death himself!
The room she sleeps in — is not this the way?
No, that way there are voices.   Am I too
    late?
Cecil . . . God guide me lest I lose the way!

                [*Exit* Elizabeth.

Cecil.

Many points weather'd, many perilous ones,
At last a harbour opens; but therein
Sunk rocks — they need fine steering — much
    it is
To be nor mad nor bigot — have a mind —
Nor let priests' talk, or dream of worlds to be,
Miscolour things about her — sudden touches
For him, or him — sunk rocks; no passionate
    faith —
But — if let be — balance and compromise;
Brave, wary, sane to the heart of her — a Tudor

School'd by the shadow of death — a Boleyn, too,
Glancing across the Tudor — not so well.

Enter ALICE.

How is the good Queen now?

ALICE.

Away from Philip.
Back in her childhood — prattling to her mother
Of her betrothal to the Emperor Charles,
And childlike-jealous of him again — and once
She thank'd her father sweetly for his book
Against that godless German. Ah, those days
Were happy.   It was never merry world
In England since the Bible came among us.

CECIL.

And who says that?

ALICE.

It is a saying among the Catholics.

CECIL.

It never will be merry world in England
Till all men have their Bible, rich and poor.

ALICE.

The Queen is dying, or you dare not say it.

Enter ELIZABETH.

ELIZABETH.

The Queen is dead.

CECIL.

Then here she stands! my homage.

ELIZABETH.

She knew me, and acknowledged me her heir,
Pray'd me to pay her debts, and keep the Faith;
Then claspt the cross, and pass'd away in
          peace.
I left her lying still and beautiful,
More beautiful than in life. Why would you
          vex yourself,
Poor sister? Sir, I swear I have no heart
To be your Queen. To reign is restless fence,
Tierce, quart, and trickery. Peace is with the
          dead.
Her life was winter, for her spring was nipt:
And she loved much: pray God she be forgiven!

CECIL.

Peace with the dead, who never were at peace!
Yet she loved one so much—I needs must
          say—

That never English monarch dying left
England so little.

ELIZABETH.

But with Cecil's aid

And others, if our person be secured
From traitor stabs — we will make England
    great.

Enter PAGET, *and other* LORDS OF THE COUNCIL,
SIR RALPH BAGENHALL, *etc.*

LORDS.

God save Elizabeth, the Queen of England!

BAGENHALL.

God save the Crown! the Papacy is no more.

PAGET (*aside*).

Are we so sure of that?

ACCLAMATION.

God save the Queen!

NOTES.

NOTES.

————————◆————————

QUEEN MARY.

'QUEEN MARY' was published in 1875, and was put upon the stage the next year at the Lyceum Theatre in London. See Vol. I. p. 92.

PAGE 11. — *And his achage.* — 'Achage' is probably Tennyson's coinage, as no other example of the word is given in the 'New English Dictionary' (Murray's).

PAGE 23. — *But does your gracious Queen entreat you king-like?* — The use of 'entreat' for 'treat' (compare Genesis, xii. 16, Exodus, v. 22, etc.) and the adverbial use of 'king-like' are both archaic.

The Game of Chess. — The capitals are Tennyson's, and suggest the double meaning of the words.

PAGE 40. — *To the Pleiads, uncle; they have lost a sister.* — The Pleiades were daughters of Atlas, placed among the stars by Jupiter, according to the familiar myth; but one of them, Electra, left her celestial station that she might not behold the ruin of Troy, which was founded by her son Dardanus.

PAGE 61. — *But his assessor in the throne.* — Literally, one who sits beside him, sharing his dignity. Compare Milton, 'Paradise Lost,' vi. 679 : —

> Whence to his Son,
> The assessor of his throne, he thus began.

PAGE 64. — *Why comes that old fox-Fleming back again?* — In the 'fox' there is a play upon the name 'Renard.' Compare page 178 below : 'But there's no Renard here,' etc.

PAGE 68. — ALINGTON CASTLE. — The ruins of this castle remain on the banks of the Medway, just below Maidstone. It was built in the reign of Stephen, and was the residence of Sir Henry Wyatt, the father of the poet. His attachment to the House of Lancaster led to his imprisonment by Richard III., but he was set free by Henry VII., and at the coronation of Henry VIII. was made a Knight of the Bath. Here Thomas Wyatt, the poet, was born in 1503. He died in 1542, leaving the estate to his son, who is introduced by Tennyson here.

PAGE 74. — *For appearance sake.* — The omission of the sign of the possessive is archaic. In Shakespeare and other Elizabethan writers it occurs even in nouns that do not end in a sibilant sound. Compare 'As You Like It,' iii. 2. 271: 'for fashion sake;' 'Twelfth Night,' iii. 4. 326: 'for's oath sake;' 'I Henry IV.' ii. 1. 78: 'for sport sake,' etc.

PAGE 109. — *Painted with the Nine Worthies.* — These famous personages were classified somewhat arbitrarily, like the Seven Wonders of the World. They were commonly said to be three Gentiles — Hector, Alexander, Julius Cæsar; three Jews — Joshua, David, Judas Maccabæus; and three Christians — Arthur, Charlemagne, Godfrey of Bouillon. In 'Love's Labour's Lost,' where they are introduced in the interlude performed by Armado, Holofernes, Sir Nathaniel, and the rest, we find Pompey and Hercules among the number.

PAGE 110. — *The tree in Virgil, etc.* — The tree that bore the golden branch. See 'Æneid,' vi. 206, etc.

PAGE 119. — *Not red like Iscariot's.* — It was a current opinion that Judas had red hair and beard, and he was commonly so represented in the old paintings and tapestries. Compare 'As You Like It,' iii. 4. 6: —

'*Rosalind.* His very hair is of the dissembling colour.

'*Celia.* Something browner than Judas's.'

See also Marston, 'The Insatiate Countess': 'I ever thought by his red beard he would prove a Judas,' etc.

PAGE 133. — *The scarlet thread of Rahab.* — See Joshua, ii. and vi.

The heathen giant. — Antæus, the son of Terra, who was invincible so long as he was in contact with the earth.

PAGE 135. — *That long low minster.* — Winchester Cathedral.

PAGE 136. — *Enclosed with boards of cedar, etc.* — See the Song of Solomon, viii. 8, 9.

PAGE 137. — *Saint Andrew's Day.* — November 30th. Compare page 146 below.

We have had it swept and garnish'd after him, etc. — See Luke, xi. 25, 26.

PAGE 141. — *Or a high-dropsy, as the doctors call it.* — The page's blunder for 'hydropsy.'

PAGE 143. — *Cocksbody.* — A corruption of 'God's body.'

PAGE 156. — *An Amphisbæna.* — A fabulous, venomous serpent supposed to have a head at each end and to be able to move in either direction. Compare Milton, 'Paradise Lost,' x. 524: 'Scorpion, and asp, and amphisbæna dire,' etc.

PAGE 158. — *Little children, Love one another.* — See 2 John, iii. 18, 23, etc.

I come not to give peace, etc. — See Matthew, x. 34.

On the steep-up track, etc. — Compare Shakespeare, Sonnet vii. 5: 'And having climb'd the steep-up heavenly hill,' etc.

PAGE 169. — *And that his fan may thoroughly purge his floor.* — See Matthew, iii. 12 or Luke, iii. 17.

PAGE 171. — *Their 'dies Iræ,' etc.* — Their judgment-day; alluding to the famous Latin hymn: 'Dies iræ, dies illa,' etc.

PAGE 174. — *Never peacock against rain, etc.* — Compare 'As You Like It,' iv. 1. 152: 'more clamorous than a parrot against rain.' Gascoigne refers to the crow in similar terms: —

> The carion Crowe, that lothsome beast,
> Which cries against the rayne.

PAGE 177. — *The lapwing lies, etc.* — Cf. 'The Comedy of Errors,' iv. 2. 27: 'Far from her nest the lapwing cries away.' This trick of the bird to divert attention from her nest became proverbial. Shakespeare alludes to it again in 'Measure for Measure,' i. 4. 32 : —

> though 't is my familiar sin
> With maids to play the lapwing and to jest,
> Tongue far from heart.

PAGE 178. — *But there's no Renard here, etc.* — See note on page 64 above.

PAGE 184. — *Mercy, that herb-of-grace.* — A figurative use of the popular name of the rue. Compare 'Hamlet,' iv. 5. 182 : 'there's rue for you ; . . . we may call it herb of grace o' Sundays ;' 'Richard II.' iii. 4. 105 : 'rue, sour herb of grace,' etc.

PAGE 189. — *You know what Virgil sings, etc.* — See the ' Æneid,' iv. 569 : 'Varium et mutabile semper Femina.'

PAGE 202. — *Martyr's blood — seed of the Church.* — The often-quoted saying of Tertullian.

PAGE 205. — *There is more joy in heaven, etc.* — See Luke, xv. 7.

PAGE 216. — *It is expedient for one man to die, etc.* — See John, xi. 50 and xviii. 14.

PAGE 218. — *To those three children, etc.* — See Daniel, iii.

PAGE 221. — *Love of this world, etc.* — See 1 John, ii. 15.

PAGE 222. — *How hard it is, etc.* — See Matthew, xix. 23, Mark, x. 23, Luke, xviii. 24.

PAGE 229. — *And Ignorance crying in the streets, etc.* — A parody on Proverbs, i. 20, 24.

PAGE 239. — *This hath offended, etc.* — An allusion to Matthew, v. 30 or Mark ix. 43.

PAGE 241. — *The narrow seas.* — The English Channel — a common name for it in that day. Compare *The Merchant of Venice*, ii. 8. 28 : —

> Who told me, in the narrow seas that part
> The French and English, there miscarried
> A vessel of our country richly fraught.

PAGE 245. — *Yet will I be your swallow and return.* — Alluding to what Mary has said (page 242) about the swallow.

PAGE 260. — *He look'd the Great Harry.* — The famous ship of war named for him.

PAGE 261. — *Have you been looking at the 'Dance of Death'?* — The separation of bridegroom and bride was represented in various forms in this series of pictures. Cf. Longfellow, 'The Golden Legend,' v. : —

> And here the heart of the new-wedded wife,
> Coming from church with her beloved lord,
> He startles with the rattle of his drum.

PAGE 269. — *They say the gloom of Saul, etc.* — See I Samuel, xvi. 23, and compare Browning's 'Saul.'

PAGE 270. — *There, am I low enough?* — Compare 'King John' (iii. 1. 73), where Constance seats herself on the ground and says : —

> Here I and Sorrow sit ;
> Here is my throne, bid kings come bow to it.

PAGE 272. — *This coarseness is a want of phantasy.* — 'Phantasy' here is equivalent to 'sensibility,' as the context indicates. It is a meaning of the word not recognised in the dictionaries.

PAGE 288. — *As in the day of the first church.* — See Acts, ii. 44 and iv. 32.

PAGE 294. — *And burn the tares with unquenchable fire.* — See Matthew, xiii. 30, 40.

Thou light a torch, etc. — Referring to Latimer's words to Ridley at the time of their martyrdom: 'We shall this day light such a candle, by God's grace, in England, as I trust shall never be put out.'

PAGE 300. — *She loved much, etc.* — See Luke, vii. 47.

END OF VOL. XI.

www.ingramcontent.com/pod-product-compliance
Lightning Source LLC
Chambersburg PA
CBHW031941080426
42735CB00007B/221